IMAGES
of Sport

MANCHESTER CITY
FOOTBALL CLUB

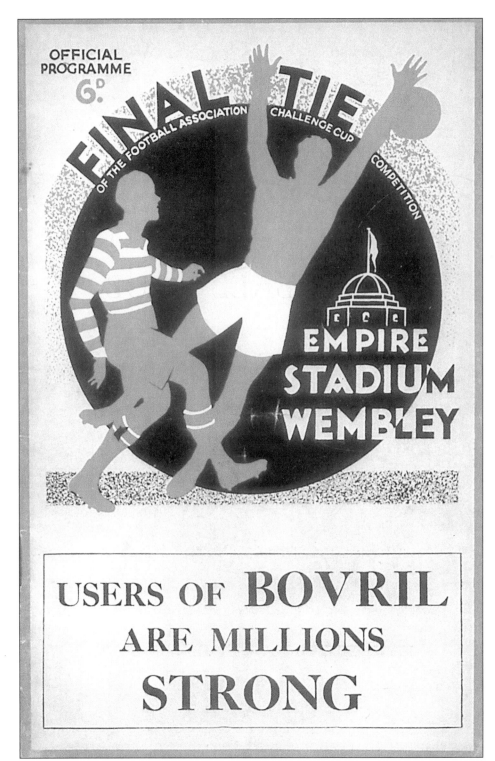

Manchester City's first victory at Wembley Stadium came in the 1934 FA Cup final when they defeated Portsmouth 2-1.

IMAGES
of Sport

MANCHESTER CITY
FOOTBALL CLUB

Compiled by
David Saffer

*To Kathleen and Roy Clarke: thanks for the chats,
coffee and especially those homemade biscuits!*

TEMPUS

First published 2000
Copyright © David Saffer, 2000

Tempus Publishing Limited
The Mill, Brimscombe Port,
Stroud, Gloucestershire, GL5 2QG

ISBN 0 7524 2085 2

Typesetting and origination by
Tempus Publishing Limited
Printed in Great Britain by
Midway Clark Printing, Wiltshire

Titles from Tempus Publishing include:

Bradford Rugby League
Castleford Rugby League
Forever England: A History of the National Side
Final Tie: The Cup Final Between the Wars
Leeds in Europe
Lords: The Cathedral of Cricket
Hampshire County Cricket Club
Ipswich Town Football Club
Salford Rugby League Club
Speedway in East Anglia
St Andrews Golfing Legends
The Five Nations Story
The Football Programme: A History and Guide
The Newcastle Rugby Story
Tottenham Hotspur Football Club 1882-1952
West Bromwich Albion Football Club
Voices of '66: Memories of England's World Cup

For a complete list of our sports titles please contact the Sales Department
(01453 883300 or sales@tempus-publishing.com).

Contents

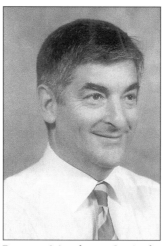

David Berstein, Manchester City's chairman.

Foreword

One's earliest experiences are often the most intense. My love affair with Manchester City began in 1954 and I was therefore extremely fortunate that within two years I had seen our club in two FA Cup finals. The first was disappointing, with that early Jackie Milburn goal and Jimmy Meadows' broken leg (there were no substitutes in those days). However, the following year on a scorching hot day in May it was a joy to see City outplay Birmingham and win the FA Cup for only the third time. Most people remember Bert Trautmann's broken neck, I will particularly recall Don Revie stepping over the ball to leave Bobby Johnstone free to score our third.

One of my next outstanding memories in the rather barren years following those Wembley appearances was seeing Dennis Law score seven goals in two FA Cup ties against Luton. Unbelievably, City would lose the tie as the first match was abandoned due to a waterlogged pitch with 15 minutes remaining as they led the game 6-2. Until recently, my most memorable moment as a City supporter was to be present at our 1-0 FA Cup semi-final win against Everton in 1969. I was sitting in line with the goal when Tommy Booth scored close to the final whistle. It was a fantastic moment with the blaze of colour from our supporters at the end the goal was scored compared with the motionless crowd at the Holt End as Everton supporters saw their cup dreams vanish.

However, I have to say that all those experiences pale against the drama of our recent victory against Gillingham. Initially I looked at that game as chairman of the club, as well as a supporter, but the drama of our late win combined with the importance of the occasion was unbeatable. I know there were tens of thousands of our fans at the match who feel exactly the same. If our recent victory at Blackburn fell slightly short in terms of last minutes drama it was nevertheless a wonderful occasion played on a hot, sunbathed pitch. It is quite something that two such recent matches compare to, and probably exceed, those earlier experiences.

Thinking about past matches is like gazing at the stars on a clear night. The longer you look the more you see and there are of course so many unforgettable games that together create our collective memory of our great club. This book contains many such glimpses into the past and I am sure that readers will find it a captivating account of the past years.

David Bernstein

The author with two of City's all-time greats: Roy Clarke and Bert Trautmann.

Introduction

This pictorial history of Manchester City Football Club aims to cover the many landmarks, achievements and personalities that have shaped this great club since its humble beginnings in 1880. To strike a sensible balance between diverse topics such as the all-time greats, championship triumphs, days of disaster, Wembley encounters and classic derby confrontations, I enlisted the help of City great Roy Clarke. Having worked on a previous book with Roy, I knew exactly what to expect – lots of laughs, plenty of tales and some expert advice.

Whilst extensive coverage is given to the Mercer/Allison era and recent events under Joe Royle, I'm particularly pleased to recall in detail the period 1880-1939. Not only did City win their first Division One title and two FA Cups, but it was also a time when the likes of Billy Meredith, Tommy Johnson, Fred Tilson, Eric Brook and Frank Swift were in their pomp.

No book on this famous club would be complete without reference to the many unforgettable encounters with our rivals from Old Trafford. Some of the historic encounters covered in this book include the City triumphs in 1955, '74 and '89. Also covered are some of those days that City fans would rather forget – Halifax in 1980, Luton in '83 and Liverpool in '89 all spring to mind. Painful though these memories are, they are as important as the days of triumph in the history of this fine old club, and so recieve their due place.

I can't let this opportunity pass without thanking David Bernstein for writing the foreword and Joe Royle, Bert Trautmann, Tony Book and Roy Clarke for allowing me to record some of their reminiscences – without their contributions the book simply wouldn't be the same.

I'm sure that when you finish reading the book you'll wonder why I missed out this game or that game or a particular player, but as I am sure you can appreciate, a book of this nature cannot feature everything. That said, I do believe that a fair representation of the club's history and some fascinating glimpses of its heritage are to be found within the selection.

I hope that you derive as much pleasure from reading it as I did from researching and compiling it.

David Saffer

City Memories

Roy Clarke

When I signed for City in 1947 they had just clinched the Championship. I was invited to a team meeting before their penultimate match of the season. I sat in the corner – there were stars everywhere. The manager, Sam Cowan, walked in. He picked up the ball, 'Hello lads', bounced the ball on the floor, 'Okay we're playing West Ham today…get stuck in', then walked out. I couldn't believe it!

Looking back, winning the FA Cup in '56 was a wonderful experience, the whole occasion…everything about it. In our day, apart from playing at Wembley in an international, the Cup Final was the only opportunity you had to play their, so after missing out in '55 through injury I was determined to savour every moment, and did. What meant most to me though was the camaraderie and banter. Players stayed for years and we were friends for life; I wouldn't change a thing.

Bert Trautmann

My debut for City was against Bolton. Frank Swift came over before the game and said 'You're playing your first League game son, ignore the crowd completely, they're not there…just concentrate'. Even in later years, I took that advice with me. Sometimes people thought I was a bit high-handed. I knew fans were there…I could hear them, but you had to stay apart – I was simply concentrating.

A few years later Germany played England, the German FA asked me to assist as an interpreter. The night before the match I stood between the posts and thought…'to play at Wembley just once'…within eighteen months I'd played there twice for City. When supporters sang *Abide with Me* you had goose pimples everywhere. The feeling inside – it's impossible to describe. City fans have always supported me, even now when I visit Maine Road or attend a function, I'm overwhelmed by the reaction supporters give me: they're truly amazing.

City Memories

Tony Book

Joe Mercer was a father figure to me, but I will always be grateful to Malcolm Allison for giving me the chance to join Manchester City and make my Division One debut at thirty-one. My years as a player were fantastic – we won every domestic honour going and triumphed in Europe too. However, if I had to pick out just one highlight it would have to be the Championship success in '68, and especially the match at Newcastle when we clinched the title. Our best player? Colin Bell – whenever I'm asked to name the best, I match up Colin against George Best…and for me Colin wins every time.

Defeating Newcastle at Wembley gave me my best moment as manager; though finishing runners-up in the League by a point the following season was a bitter disappointment. Even so, I've been very fortunate.

Joe Royle

My time as a City player meant an awful lot to me. The team had been rebuilt after their heady days in the late '60s and early '70s when they were one of the teams to beat. Nevertheless, with Joe Corrigan, Willie Donachie, Dave Watson, Asa Hartford and Dennis Tueart in our side we could give anyone a game…and did. The highlight? Our League Cup final win over Newcastle in '76, because as a player it was the only time I won a winners medal at Wembley.

Moving on to more recent times, the last two seasons have been a bit of a roller-coaster ride to say the least, and certainly our victories at Wembley and Blackburn will take some beating. However, now we're back in the Premier League we must look forward and give our magnificent supporters something to really shout about.

Roll of Honour

Division One
1937, 1968

Division Two
1899, 1903, 1910, 1928, 1947, 1966

European Cup-Winners' Cup
1970

FA Cup
1904, 1934, 1956, 1969

Football League Cup Winners
1970, 1976

FA Charity Shield
1937, 1968, 1972

FA Youth Challenge Cup
1986

Acknowledgements

I would like to thank all of the following individuals and organisations for their help with this publication: David Bernstein, Roy Clarke, Joe Royle, Bert Trautmann, Tony Book, Manchester City Football Club, James Howarth and Chris Mason at Tempus Publishing, Andrew Waldon and Leon Phillips.

A sincere thanks also to the *Manchester Evening News* for supplying many of the images in this book, and especially to Fay Walter in the syndication department for her help and patience! Whilst every attempt has been made to acknowledge the original source of copyright for all pictures in this publication, if anyone has any questions relating to this matter please contact Tempus Publishing.

Andrew Waldon has kindly supplied all the statistics relating to player appearances and goals. They appear in the following format: total matches played (substitute appearances), for example, Alan Oakes 676 (4). Where a player never made a substitute appearance their details appear as follows: Eric Brook 493.

One
In the Beginning

Formed in 1880 as St Mark's of West Gorton, the club changed its name to West Gorton (St Mark's) in 1881, Gorton in 1884 and then Ardwick in 1887, before bankruptcy in 1894 led to the formation of Manchester City Football Club. Unsurprisingly, the changes in personnel and administration led to the team's home ground constantly changing. Venues included Clowes Street, Kirkmanhulme Cricket Club, Clemington Street, Pink Bank Lane, and Reddish Lane, before eventually settling at Hyde Road in 1887. This photograph shows the Manchester City side of around 1900.

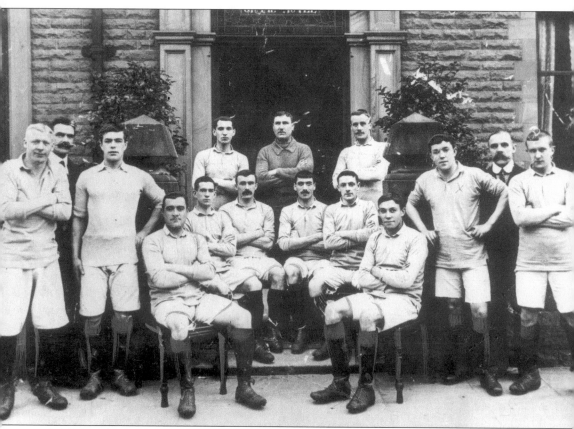

St Mark's of West Gorton played their first match on 13 November 1880 against Baptist Church (Macclesfield), and the result was a 2-1 win for Baptist. For eleven years the team played friendly matches or entered local cup competitions. Lawrence Furniss was Ardwick's first secretary-manager in 1889 and during his tenure Ardwick won the Manchester Cup in consecutive seasons. These results helped the club gain entry to the Football Alliance in 1891 and Division Two of the Football League twelve months later. In their debut season in the Football League, 1892/93, Ardwick began by defeating Bootle 7-0 and they ended the campaign in fifth place. Joshua Parlby succeeded Furniss in 1893, becoming the club's first paid secretary, though Furniss would stay for a further forty-six years, serving as both chairman and club president. In 1893/94, City lost 2-10 to Small Heath and twelve months later they defeated Lincoln City 11-3 – both results still stand as club records for a League game. The 1894/95 season also marked the debut of Billy Meredith, City's most influential player over the next decade. Sam Ormerod replaced Parlby in 1895 and oversaw City's first Division Two title success in 1898/99. Of their 23 wins that season, the most emphatic was a 10-0 triumph over Darwen (F. Williams scoring 5 goals and Meredith 3). The team scored 92 goals in total, Meredith top-scoring with 29 (including 4 hat-tricks). City lost their top-flight status in 1901/02, but returned immediately as champions under new secretary-manager Tom Maley. This time City won 25 matches, scoring 95 goals, including 35 in a six-game scoring-blitz against: Chesterfield 4-2, Burnley 6-0, Burslem Port Vale 7-1, Small Heath 4-0, Gainsborough Town 9-0 and Burton United 5-0. Top scorer was bustling centre forward Billy Gillespie with 30. The leading scorer between 1902 and 1904, Gillespie thrived on the service Meredith provided, and struck 132 goals in his 231 appearances for the club. This photograph shows Manchester City at the beginning of the twentieth century in front of the Grand Hotel.

Billy Meredith before a match in 1900. An FA Cup-winner with City in 1904, Meredith was adept at firing in pinpoint crosses or cutting in from the right flank to score. Following a suspension in 1905 for allegedly bribing a player, he joined Manchester United, returning in 1921. He finally retired at the grand old age of fifty. The club's top scorer five times, he struck 151 goals in 393 appearances for City and won 48 Welsh caps. A champion of footballers' rights, Billy Meredith was a real 'great' of Edwardian football.

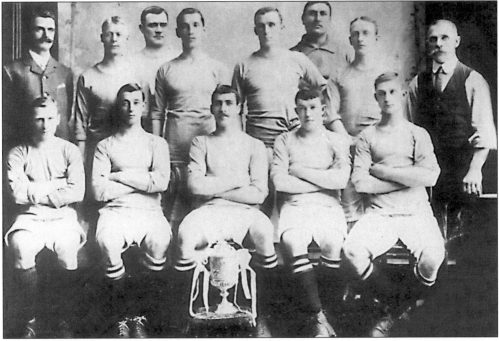

In 1903/04 Manchester City reached the FA Cup final for the first time, following victories over Sunderland 3-2, Woolwich Arsenal 2-0, Middlesborough 3-1, and Sheffield Wednesday 3-1. In the final they defeated Bolton Wanderers 1-0, Meredith scoring a disputed goal. This photograph shows the team (Hillman, McMahon, Burgess, Frost, Hynds, Ashworth, Meredith, Livingstone, Gillespie, Turnbull and Booth) displaying the trophy. Meredith is seated behind the FA Cup, whilst Tom Maley is on the extreme left of the back row. Within two seasons both would depart: Meredith due to the bribe scandal, Maley for his part in an illegal payments scandal, in which the FA suspended him and chairman Mr Forest *sine die*. In addition, other players and directors received hefty fines and suspensions before also departing.

Manchester City FC, 1906/07. From left to right, back row: Baldwin, Smith, Buchan, Norgrove, Eadie, Steele, Davies, Hill, Kelso, Evans, Taylor. Front row: Whittaker, Hamblett, Grieve, Christie, Conlin, Young, Banks, Stewart. Seated: Thornley, Fisher, Dorsett. This squad was put together by Harry Newbould in the aftermath of Maley's departure. After avoiding relegation, they finished third the following term, but any hopes of another title challenge soon faded twelve months later when the team dropped into Division Two.

Manchester City FC, 1908/09. From left to right, inset: Dorsett, Broomfield, Stewart, Jackson, Eadie. Back row: Newbould (secretary-manager), Wilkinson (chairman), Hancock, Kelso, Coupe, Davies, Burgess, Wilkinson, Grieve, Buchan, Chait (trainer). Front row: Smith, Thornley, Jones, Holford, Ross, Conlin, Blair. Newbould's squad regained top-flight status immediately, but two seasons of relegation battles took their toll. Newbould could offer no more and Ernest Mangnall became manager in September 1912. Of this 1908/09 squad, George Dorsett (211, 65 goals), Bill Eadie (205), Walter Smith (256), Billy Lot Jones (302, 74 goals) and Irvine Thornley (204, 93 goals) would all play over 200 games for the club. In addition, Thornley would top-score four times in his nine seasons with the club.

Prior to the First World War, Ernest Mangnall led City to two top-six finishes, though his side did struggle at times in attack. On resumption of League football in 1919 this would change when Horace Barnes and Tommy Browell teamed up. For three seasons they were unstoppable; sharing 133 goals (Browell 74, Barnes 59), and in 1920/21 City just missed out on attaining their first Division One title, finishing runners-up to Burnley. This is the 1919/20 squad. From left to right, back row: Sharp, Broad (trainer), Mangnall (secretary), Goodchild, Woosnam (captain), Allen, Godfrey, Tyler. Front row: Cookson, Broad, Browell, Johnson, Barnes, Cartwright. Full-back Eli Fletcher – one of the club's longest serving players, with a total of 326 appearances – is missing from this picture.

Horace Barnes came from Derby County in May 1914 for £2,500 and had the honour of scoring City's first ever goal at Maine Road on 25 August 1923 *v.* Sheffield United. Barnes had a fierce left-foot shot and created havoc when in partnership with Tommy Browell. He struck a total of 125 goals in his 235 appearances for the club.

Tommy 'Boy' Browell was a natural goalscorer. Indeed, in 1910 Hull City's directors were so keen to sign him that they rowed across the Tyne to contact him at his home village…and succeeded. Later that year, after scoring a hat-trick, one journalist commented that 'ten men and a boy beat Stockport'. Following a spell at Everton, City paid £1,780 in 1913 for his goal-scoring prowess and he went on to forge a deadly partnership with Horace Barnes. Browell scored 139 goals in 247 appearances for City, and was unfortunate not to be capped by England.

Hyde Road had been City's home ground since 1887, but after the main stand burnt down in November 1920 moves intensified for a new site. City finally left in 1923 for their new home at Maine Road, winning the opening match there against Sheffield United 2-1. Though they finished the 1923/24 campaign in eleventh place, they did reach the semi-finals of the FA Cup, in which Billy Meredith, then aged fifty, played. David Ashworth, who had surprisingly left Liverpool in February 1923 having guided them to the League Championship in 1921/22, was in charge of the team at this time. When Barnes moved to Preston, Frank Roberts, who had signed for City in 1922 for £3,400 from Bolton, took over in attack and top-scored in 1924/25 with 31 goals. During his time at City, Roberts, who won four England caps, mainly partnered Tommy Johnson in attack, and struck 130 goals in his 237 appearances. In 1925/26, Browell, Roberts and Johnson struck 57 goals but their efforts were wasted as the defence leaked 100 of them, resulting in relegation once again. This demise brought about a change in manager – Peter Hodge replacing Ashworth. This is City's line-up before Ashworth's departure. From left to right, back row: Cookson, Mitchell, Thompson, Cowan, Bell (trainer). Front row: Ashworth (manager), Sharp, Austin, Dennison, Roberts, Pringle, Johnson, Hicks. Jimmy McMullan, arguably Scotland's best left-half of the era, is missing from the photograph. Skipper of the 'Wembley Wizards' who trounced England 5-1 in 1928, Jimmy played in two Cup Finals for City during an eight-year spell in which he made 242 appearances, scoring 12 times.

Tommy 'Tosh' Johnson still holds City's club record for scoring the most League goals in a season with 38 in 1928/29, and his total figure of 166 in 354 matches places him second on the all-time scorers' list at Maine Road. Recommended by Eli Fletcher, who refused to re-sign unless Johnson was signed up, Tommy gave magnificent service during his eleven seasons at the club. His most prolific season came in 1928/29 when he scored a club record 38 League goals, including five at Everton in a 6-2 win. Surprisingly for such a prolific scorer, Tommy was top scorer for City on just one other occasion, when he struck 25 goals in 1926/27, but nothing can detract from this potent striker who reached double figures on no fewer than five occasions. Many supporters criticised the board when they let him go to Everton, especially when he was in the Everton side that defeated City in the 1933 FA Cup final. Johnson played in the 1926 Cup Final at Wembley for City and gained two of his five England caps whilst at Maine Road.

Sam Cookson was arguably the best full-back of his era not to gain full international honours. Though of stocky build, any winger who believed they could skip past him soon respected his skills. Cookson played a total of 306 matches, scoring just once in a 3-3 draw with Corinthians during City's 1926 FA Cup run.

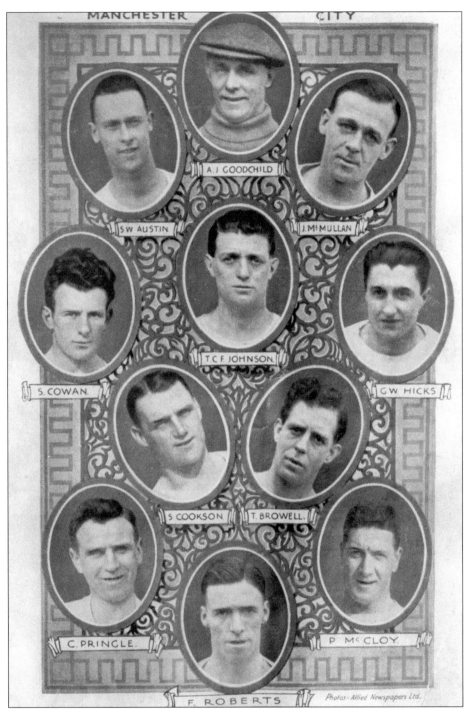

A consolation for the team in 1926 was their first FA Cup final appearance at Wembley following victories over Corinthians 4-0 (after a 2-2 draw), Huddersfield 4-0, Crystal Palace 11-4 (Roberts 5 goals, Browell 3 goals), Clapton 6-1 and Manchester United 3-0. This is City's FA Cup final team: Goodchild, Cookson, McCloy, Pringle, Cowan, McMullan, Austin, Browell, Roberts, Johnson and Hicks.

City's skipper is introduced to King George V prior to the final with Bolton Wanderers.

Action at the City end during the final.

More action, but this time from City's attack – the 'keeper under pressure (above and below) is Pym in the Bolton goal. Sadly, City lost to a single David Jack strike.

City lost out in the race for promotion in 1926/27 by 1/200th of a goal, despite scoring 108 goals and winning their last game of the season 8-0! Still, they made sure twelve months later when they struck another century of goals, Johnson and Roberts scoring 39 between them. The pair shared a further 39 the following term before Johnson scored his club record 38 League goals in 1928/29 – including five at Everton in a 6-2 win. The next decade would begin with City finishing third, although it was the FA Cup that would dominate the early '30s as far as City were concerned. In 1931/32 City reached the semi-finals before being thwarted by Arsenal. By the start of their next tilt at the FA Cup, Wilf Wild had replaced Hodge and within months they had reached Wembley following victories over Gateshead 9-0 (after a 1–1 draw), Walsall 2-0, Bolton 4-2, Burnley 1-0 and Derby 3-2. Unfortunately, as in 1926 it would end in heartache, Everton winning 3-0 with the legendary Dixie Dean scoring for the Toffeemen. City's team consisted of: Langford, Cann, Dale, Busby, Cowan, Bray, Toseland, Marshall, Herd, McMullan, Brook. In 1933/34 the players once again reached Wembley after wins over Blackburn 3-1, Hull City 4-1 and Sheffield Wednesday 2-0 (following a couple of 2-2 draws), Stoke City 1-0 and Aston Villa 6-1 (Fred Tilson scoring four times in the match). This photograph shows City players relaxing at the Palace Hotel before the 1934 Cup Final.

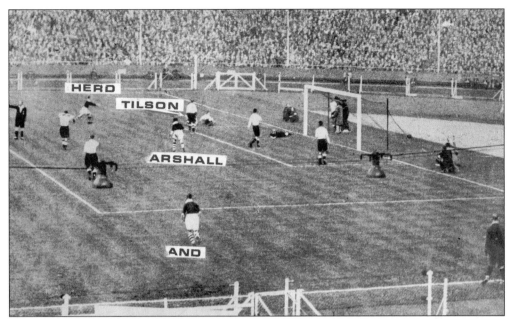

City came back from going a goal behind in the final to defeat Portsmouth 2-1, Tilson scoring twice in the last twenty minutes. At the final whistle a young Frank Swift, just six months into his City career in goal, was so overcome by emotion that he fainted! City's victorious line-up consisted of: Swift, Barnett, Dale, Busby, Cowan, Bray, Toseland, Marshall, Tilson, Herd, Brook.

Sam Cowan holds aloft the FA Cup during the team's homecoming. A stopper centre-half, Cowan joined City from Doncaster Rovers in 1924 (the year he was credited with scoring a hat-trick of headers for the South Yorkshire side in their game against Halifax). During his eleven seasons at Maine Road he played in three FA Cup finals and scored 24 goals in 407 appearances. He also won two England caps. Cowan later managed City, steering them to promotion in 1946/47.

Manchester City proudly display the FA Cup in 1934. From left to right, back row (directors): R. Smith, W. Shaw, H. Wood, Dr J. Holmes. Third row: W. Wild (secretary-manager), A. Alexander (director), M. Busby, F. Swift, L. Barnett, J. Bray, A. Bell (trainer). Second row: F. Tilson, W. Dale, S. Cowan (captain), A. Hughes (chairman), R. Marshall, A. Herd, J. McLuckie. Front row (on ground): E. Toseland, E. Brook.

Fred Tilson formed a wonderful partnership with Eric Brook down the left flank. Both had joining City from Barnsley in a joint £6,000 fee. During his time at Maine Road, Tilson won League and FA Cup winners medals, scoring both goals in the 1934 FA Cup final. In all Tilson scored 132 goals in 275 appearances for City, and won 4 England caps, scoring 6 times for this country. After he retired from playing, Fred returned to Maine Road to serve successfully as a coach, assistant manager and chief scout.

Eric Brook, City's most prolific striker, signed from Barnsley with Fred Tilson and became a vital member of the City team in the 1930s. An unorthodox outside left, Brook would come off both flanks – creating panic in opposing defences. A great passer of the ball, Eric had a thunderous shot and was an expert penalty taker. As City's record goal scorer (177) – not to mention being sixth on the all-time appearances list (493) – his achievement is unlikely to be beaten. Eric showed great versatility by playing at full-back and even deputised in goal on three occasions. An England international, his total of 16 caps would have been higher if it had not been for Arsenal's Cliff Bastin.

City finished fifth in 1933/34, despite a 0-8 mauling at Wolves and a 2-7 reverse at home to West Brom. Alex Herd top scored for the first time with 17 goals (repeating the feat in 1938/39 with 20). A deep-lying inside forward, Herd not only struck 125 goals in his 288 appearances but also created countless others with his great dribbling ability. City came fourth the following term but would have finished higher had they not lost four of their final five fixtures. Tilson (18), Brook (17), Herd (14) and Heale (13) accounted for the majority of City's 82 league goals, and amongst twenty victories were two consecutive six-goal wins against Leicester 6-3 and Middlesborough 6-2. Unsurprisingly, the players had high hopes for the 1935/36 campaign, especially after gaining five wins in there opening six matches. However, ten defeats in eighteen ended any hope of League success. Reinforcements were needed and Wilf Wild made what would prove to be his most inspirational signing…Blackpool's Peter Doherty. His arrival not only brought stability, as City ended the season ninth, but would prove the catalyst for City's first Division One title. Above is City's squad in 1935/36 prior to Doherty's arrival. From left to right, back row: Chorlton (trainer), Dale, Busby, Cowan, Swift, Donnelly, Bray, Percival, Barkas, Barnett (assistant trainer). Front row: Dellow, Marshall, Toseland, Herd, Heale, Tilson, Brook. Of this experienced squad Cowan, Swift, Marshall, Toseland and Brook would each make over 350 appearances, whilst Billy Dale (271), Sam Barkas (195), Jackie Bray (279), Matt Busby (227) and Alec Herd (288) would all serve the club with distinction. Amazingly, the team's brilliant inside right, Bobby Marshall, ended the season as City's first choice centre half! This may sound strange, but Marshall had in fact made occasional appearances in the position previously, due to injuries. His versatility not only extended his career at City, but resulted in him somewhat unusually gaining a Cup winners' medal playing on the right flank and a Championship medal playing in defence. In all he appeared 356 times for City, scoring 80 goals. Another key member of City's successful side of the 1930s was Ernie Toseland. Rarely missing a match throughout his eleven seasons at Maine Road, this flying winger appeared in 411 matches, scoring 75 goals.

Frank Swift was a cheeky, larger than life goalkeeper, who signed for City in the autumn of 1932. After making his debut against Derby on Christmas Day 1933, Swift appeared in every League game for over four seasons, and missed just one game during the 1938/39 season when City were defeated 1-6 at home by Millwall. In total Frank made 375 appearances for the club, but would probably have broken the club's appearance record had the war years not cost him seven seasons. He totally dominated his goal area, his 12-inch finger-span allowing him to grasp the ball one-handed. Unlike most 'keepers of his era, Swift elected to throw the ball to colleagues rather than hoof the ball downfield. Frank won First and Second Championship medals for City, in addition to an FA Cup winners' medal in 1934 when just nineteen years of age. After the final, in which he famously fainted due to the relief and excitement of winning, he commented somewhat embarrassingly: 'Fancy a great strapping fellow like me fainting in front of all those people and the King!' Although he played his last match for the club in 1949, City held on to his registration until 1955. Frank deservedly won 16 caps for England and in 1948 he became the first goalkeeper to captain his country. Tragically, he died in the Munich air disaster whilst covering the match as a reporter. One of the best 'keepers of his or any era, Frank Swift was one of City's all-time greats.

In 1936/37 City became Division One Champions for the first time, underpinned by a remarkable sequence of twenty-two matches in which they were unbeaten, including consecutive victories over: Liverpool (5-1), Brentford (6-2 and 2-1), Arsenal (2-0), Sunderland (3-1), Preston (5-2), and Sheffield Wednesday (4-1). Their record for the season was: played 42, won 22, drawn 13 and lost 7; goals for 107, goals against 61; 57 points. Top scorers were Doherty (30) and Brook (20), while Swift, Percival, Toseland and Brook were ever-present in the side. City's key player was probably Doherty. Signed in 1936, he was often described as 'the greatest player produced by Ireland'. Tactically brilliant, he was the complete footballer. In addition to his 16 caps, he managed Northern Ireland to the 1958 World Cup quarter-finals. Doherty played 131 matches for City, scoring 81 goals.

City went on a post-season tour of Germany after their success, yet within a season were relegated. Typically they did it in style – scoring more goals than anyone else did! Their victims in this ultimately disastrous campaign included: Derby 7-1, West Brom 7-1 and Leeds 6-2. Twelve months on they finished fifth in the final season before the Second World War. This photograph shows the players on a break whilst touring. From left to right: Doherty, Marshall, Herd, Bray (hidden), Toseland, Dale, Swift, Brook, Barkas and Tilson.

Two
Halcyon Days

When the Football League returned to some semblance of normality in 1946, only Barkas, Swift and Herd remained from the 1937 Championship team. City began with four wins in six matches, but by autumn Wild had reverted to secretarial duties with Sam Cowan becoming manager. The players were clearly unaffected as they embarked on an unbeaten twenty-two-match run, with seventeen wins, that clinched yet another Division Two title. Top scorer was Black with 23 goals. When promotion was settled City strengthened their squad by purchasing Roy Clarke. His debut in the last match against Newport County was sanctioned because the result had no bearing on relegation. The match, delayed due to a severe winter, saw George Smith score all City's goals in a 5-1 win. This photograph shows Roy being welcomed to the club by manager Sam Cowan on 23 May 1947.

The players line up before their opening fixture of the 1947/48 season at Wolves. From left to right, back row: Fagan, Sprotson, unknown, Swift, Westwood, Emtage. Front row: Wharton, Black, McMorran, McDowell, Smith. A regular scorer for City during the early post-war years was George Smith, who struck 80 goals in 179 appearances: of this side only Frank Swift and full-back Eric Westwood would play more times – Westwood making a total of 260 appearances in his nine seasons at the club.

Clarke, Wharton and McMorran before a thriller with Wolves which City edged 4-3, Clarke scoring the deciding goal. By November 1947 Jack Thomson had replaced Sam Cowan as manager, due to the board's concern over Cowan's continued practise of commuting from his home in Hove. City ended the season in tenth place.

February 1948, and it's special training on the beach in Blackpool prior to an FA Cup clash with Preston. Unfortunately the preparation didn't work, Preston winning 1-0.

The City line-up prior to their biggest win of the 1948/49 season – a 4-1 success at home to Aston Villa in which George Smith grabbed a hat-trick. From left to right, back row: Barnett (trainer), Smith, Westwood, Sprotson, Swift, Fagan, Walsh, unknown. Front row: Oakes, Black, McDowell, Linacre, Clarke.

It is 27 November 1948, and Derby are beaten 2-1 with this strike from Roy Clarke – one of 79 goals in his 370 appearances on the left flank. Roy also gained 22 caps for Wales. His debut against Newport formed part of a unique record in which Roy played in three Football League divisions in consecutive matches: Cardiff City's penultimate Division Three match in 1946/47, City's final Division Two clash *v.* Newport, and their opening Division One fixture at Wolves the following term. A member of City's 1956 FA Cup-winning side, Roy finished his playing days at Stockport County, before setting up and running the commercial department and social club at Maine Road for many years. Apart from helping to establish the Ex-players Association, he still acts as president of Manchester City Supporters Club (1949) and regularly entertains guests on match days.

Players and officials depart on a post-season tour of Denmark in May 1949. The team won three out of their six matches abroad.

As the team approached a new decade they could be forgiven for feeling reasonably confident after the last two campaigns. Unfortunately, just eight victories – their worst haul ever in a forty-two match season – meant Division Two football again. This photograph shows Clarke heading just wide as City crash 0-3 at home to Blackpool on 24 September 1949.

Another defeat, this time 3-5 to Derby County in an FA Cup third round clash at Maine Road. City also lost their away League clash with the Rams 7-0, so it's safe to assume this was one team they were happy to avoid in Division Two!

Relegation saw a change in management with ex-City half-back Les McDowell beginning what would be a thirteen-year tenure. *Above*: Pre-season 1950/51 and the players prepare themselves at Butlin's holiday camp in Filey. *Below*: They continue the hard slog back at Maine Road.

The opening match in 1950/51 saw the debuts of Roy Paul and Johnny Hart. Both would make vital contributions as City clinched promotion at the first attempt. The goals flowed, with Westcott, Smith and Hart sharing 60 of City's 89 League goals. In this shot Clarke is all smiles with Paul on 12 October 1950. The two would play much of the decade together for City and Wales.

The players line up before a League clash with Brentford on 10 October 1950. Goals from Westcott (2), Hart and Clarke gave City a 4-0 win. From left to right, back row: Westcott, Phillips, Spurdle, Trautmann, Westwood, Rigby. Front row: Alison, Hart, Paul (captain), Smith, Clarke.

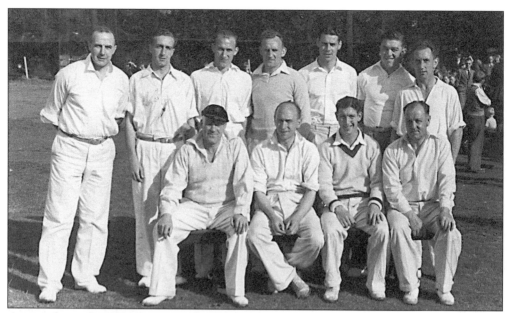

Anyone for cricket! Players past and present are in this City line-up from around 1951. On the front row (extreme left and extreme right) are City legends Eric Brook and Fred Tilson.

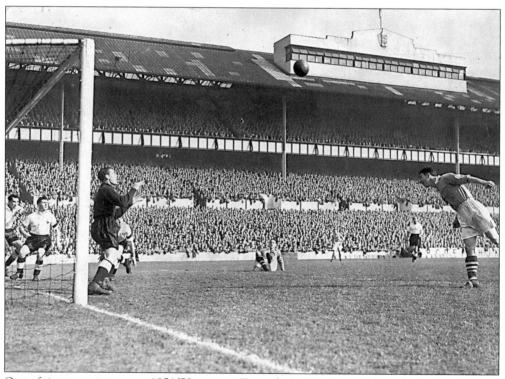

One of six away victories in 1951/52 came at Tottenham, Clarke grabbing a brace in a 2-1 win. Unfortunately, home form let the team down and with just seven victories at Maine Road City finished the season in fifteenth place.

City just avoided relegation in 1952/53 after some poor displays, best illustrated at Wolves (3-7), Preston (2-6), and Derby County (0-5). Performances carried on in a similar manner the following term as City stumbled to seventeenth place. *Above:* Clarke attempts to break through the Wolves rearguard; he was unsuccessful as City went down 0-4 on August 1953. *Below:* The players pose for photographers prior to a match in 1954.

In 1954/55 the first team employed a new tactic – the Revie plan. Ken Barnes played a key role and he recalls that 'Les McDowell experimented with different formations, but the most famous became known as the Revie plan. Originally I played this system in the reserves with Johnny Williamson; we didn't lose for thirty-odd games. The first team tried it at the start of '54/55 at Preston; we lost 0-5! However, we persevered and it brought a lot of success. Defences were used to a big centre forward like Nat Lofthouse or Trevor Ford staying up, it was a real battle. Against us our centre forward, Don Revie, would play deeper and come at them; not be with them all the time, so the centre-halves had nobody to mark. We played the ball in the middle of the park and started linking up. Don, me at wing half, our inside forwards and wingers would alternate and it caused problems. When I was running towards our box and saw the ball coming over I knew Bert would gather it so I'd turn the other way to attack. Bert would come out "here have it" and I'd be on my way linking up. Going forward with the attack was a piece of cake as far as I was concerned. I loved the system'. This photograph shows Roy Clarke, together with the original exponents of the Revie plan – Johnny Williamson and, of course, Don Revie – leave Maine Road following a match in 1954.

Manchester City FC, *c.* 1955.

The most pleasing results of the 1954/55 season? That's easy as this season contained the first League double over Manchester United since 1930/31 – 3-2 at home and 5-0 at Old Trafford. City also beat United 2-0 in the FA Cup, which was the first time that either neighbour had won three derbies in a season. In this picture Clarke jumps over Revie's goal-bound shot that gave City a two-goal cushion in the cup clash with United. (Note: this treble has only occurred twice in the club's history, Joe Mercer's 1969/70 squad matching the achievement.)

The semi-final would bring both elation and heartbreak for Roy Clarke. Elation because his goal sent the team to Wembley, but also heartbreak because an injury would cost him his place in the final itself. Here, Wally Barnes and John Mctavish help Roy from the field after he sustained his injury.

OFFICIAL PROGRAMME

THE FOOTBALL ASSOCIATION
CHALLENGE CUP

SEMI-FINAL TIE

Photograph by A. Wilkes & Son, West Bromwich.

MANCHESTER CITY
v.
SUNDERLAND

VILLA PARK, BIRMINGHAM
SATURDAY, MARCH 26th 1955
KICK-OFF 2-30 p.m.

PRICE 6 D. ISSUED BY
ASTON VILLA F.C.

Apart from the United treble, there was a bonus of a trip to Wembley in the FA Cup following victories over Derby 3-1, Manchester United 2-0, Luton 2-0, Birmingham 1-0 and Sunderland 1-0. This is the semi-final match programme with Sunderland.

Roy Clarke organises Cup Final
memorabilia in his sports shop during the
build up to the final.

The official FA Cup final brochure.
City's team in the 1955 Cup Final lined
up as follows: Trautmann, Meadows,
Little, Barnes, Ewing, Paul, Spurdle,
Hayes, Revie, Johnstone, Fagan.

The Duke of Edinburgh chats with Don Revie prior to the Wembley clash with Newcastle on 7 May 1955.

Jimmy Schoular and Roy Paul shake hands before the final. The referee is Reg Leafe.

A goal down within a minute, City never recovered when Jimmy Meadows departed through injury after just twenty minutes. Despite a Bobby Johnstone equaliser, the ten men of City went down 3-1. After the defeat Roy Paul vowed City would be back twelve months later...but with a different result. *Above*: Trautmann stops Vic Keeble in his tracks. *Below*: Johnstone briefly raised hopes with this scorching strike.

Ex-coal-miner Roy Paul joined City from Swansea Town in July 1950 for £25,000. A hard working and talented half-back, Paul was a tremendous motivator and a regular throughout his City career. As skipper he captained the team to their Division Two and FA Cup successes of the 1950s. In all he made 294 appearances in City's colours, scoring 9 times. He also won 33 caps for Wales. In a recent poll to decide the greatest skipper in the club's history, Roy Paul was a clear winner.

Ken Barnes was often described as being 'the best-uncapped wing-half of his era'. A skilful and consistent player, Ken joined City in May 1950 from Stafford Rangers but had to wait until the mid-1950s before becoming a regular in the side, a position he held for the next seven seasons, appearing in two FA Cup finals for the club. After retiring as a player he returned as a coach before becoming the club's chief scout. Barnes played 283 games in all, scoring 19 goals.

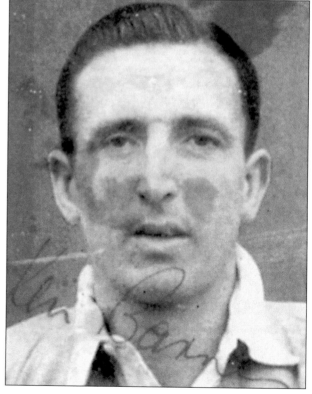

Don Revie signed in 1951 from Hull City for £25,000 and is remembered by City fans as the tactical architect of the Revie plan. His best season came in 1954/55 when he guided City to FA Cup glory and won the Footballer of the Year award. Though not assured of his place in the side, he returned to Wembley in 1956 to give a virtuoso performance. He left shortly after and went on to manage Leeds United and England. He played a total of 178 times for City, scoring 41 goals.

Bert Trautmann arrived in England in April 1945. He started his career at St Helens Town before signing for City in November 1949. He had to overcome supporters' resentment because of his nationality but soon won the hearts of all City followers. He was voted Footballer of the Year in 1956, a season in which he famously broke his neck making a heroic save in the Cup Final. Acknowledged as a legend at the club, Bert is one of only four players to have played over 500 times for Manchester City and currently stands fourth on the all-time appearances list, having played in 545 matches for the club.

Above: Pre-season was as hard as ever, even if the players seem quite relaxed during circuit training. *Left*: Four benches are no problem for Roy Paul and Ken Barnes.

The Blues Brothers! City trainer Laurie Barnett supervises deep heat treatment for Roy Clarke and Don Revie.

The trappings of success...new boots from the sponsors! Despite a slow start City had their best season for years, finishing fourth, with Joe Hayes top scoring on 23 goals.

Above: Manchester City FC, 1955/56. As Roy Paul had promised, City returned to Wembley following victories over Blackpool 2-1, Southend 2-1, Liverpool 2-1 (after a 2-2 draw), Everton 2-1, and Tottenham 1-0. Bobby Johnstone scored 50 goals for City in 139 appearances, but the one he scored against Tottenham in the semi-final was by far his most important. *Below*: The players limber up for the final with a spot of tug-o'-war on 23 April 1956.

Before departing for their pre-Wembley preparations, confectioner Harold Kinder and *Evening News* reader Mr Skitt presented Roy Paul with this good luck gift.

City's 1956 Cup Final team…or is it? Note the absence of Don Revie, who would come in as an eleventh-hour replacement when Bill Spurdle was forced to pull out through injury. Taking his favoured deep-lying role, Bobby Johnstone was switched to outside-right. The actual eleven on the day was: Trautmann, Leivers, Little, Barnes, Ewing, Paul, Johnstone, Hayes, Revie, Dyson, Clarke.

THE FOOTBALL ASSOCIATION CHALLENGE CUP COMPETITION

FINAL TIE

BIRMINGHAM CITY
v
MANCHESTER CITY

SATURDAY, MAY 5th, 1956   KICK-OFF 3 pm

EMPIRE STADIUM

WEMBLEY

Chairman and Managing Director   SIR ARTHUR J. ELVIN, MBE
OFFICIAL PROGRAMME   ONE SHILLING

The match programme for the Manchester City *v*. Birmingham City FA Cup final. There was only going to be one outcome to this match, as Clarke recalls, 'Before the game we were more relaxed than in '55... we knew what to expect. They didn't have any really classy footballers like us and our movement on the pitch suited Wembley. During the team talk Les McDowell reminded us not to "carry the ball too much", because the pitch could sap your energy, he emphasised "tire the ball out...not yourselves". Then it was time to go. When we left the dressing room I knew we'd go back as winners. In the tunnel I was behind Roy as usual...he was really fired up...I can still see him shaking his fist to encourage us, I think it unnerved their players!'

Roy Paul leads the team out prior to the final with Birmingham City.

As in 1955 The Duke of Edinburgh was guest of honour. *Above*: The Duke being introduced to Bert Trautmann. *Below*: Within minutes City were ahead through a Joe Hayes strike – and what a goal it was! Clarke recalls the moment: 'Joe's goal was a shining example of the Revie plan. Bert moved the ball to Don via Bill Leivers and Ken Barnes. Don then played it forty yards to me, shouting "Hang on", because he wanted the return. Their full-back was coming over and I thought "Come on Don…". He went past me and I played the ball just inside a diagonal to him. He ran over it and flicked it between his legs to Joe Hayes who knocked it in the far corner…so simple, yet brilliant.'

Even though Birmingham equalised the players knew they had the beating of their opponents and further strikes by Jack Dyson (above, wheeling away after scoring) and Bobby Johnstone (below) gave City a comfortable 3-1 victory. The match had a final twist near the end when Bert Trautmann heroically played on unaware he had broken his neck following a number of brave saves.

The Queen congratulates Roy Paul
on the club's success before
presenting him with the FA Cup.

Delighted supporters congratulate
their heroes as they descend from
the Royal Box with the trophy.

Bert Trautmann is helped from the field clearly suffering. It would be a few days before he would know the full extent of his injury. Bert recalled: 'After the match no doctor examined my neck, I felt as if I had toothache! On the Sunday I went to St George's Hospital in Kensington and the junior doctors were on. I had an X-ray, they said I'd ricked my neck!'

What do you think to this son…?

Roy Paul delivers his promise…

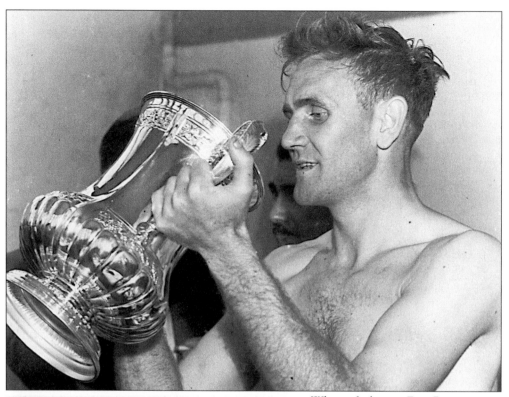

What a feeling as Don Revie experiences the sweet taste of victory.

Time to depart for home after a job well done.

The victorious team is escorted through Manchester city centre after their triumph.

Manchester City FC, FA Cup winners, 1956. From left to right, back row: W. Griffiths (secretary), A. Douglas, R. Smith, W. Smith, F. Jolly, E. Gill (all directors). Middle row: Laurie Barnett (trainer), Ken Barnes, Bill Leivers, Bert Trautmann, Dave Ewing, Roy Little, Les McDowell (manager). Front row: Bobby Johnstone, Joe Hayes, Roy Paul (captain), Don Revie, Jack Dyson, Roy Clarke.

Joe Hayes allegedly arrived for a trial game at City with his boots in a brown paper parcel. He scored four goals and weeks later made his League debut. A tremendous opportunist in front of goal, his prolific marksmanship would have been far greater had it not been for a serious knee injury in 1964. Fourth on the club's all-time scoring list with 152 goals, Joe appeared in 364 matches for City.

Dave Ewing was the anchor of the defence that helped City win the FA Cup in 1956. A tall, vocal, strong centre-half, he formed a formidable partnership with half-backs Paul and Barnes. Ewing later became a coach at City, running the reserve team that won the title in 1977/78 for the first time in the club's history. Dave made 303 appearances, scoring just once against Portsmouth in 1957.

Bill Leivers was a centre-half playing for Chesterfield when City paid £10,500 for him in November 1953. His defensive skills and commitment deserved greater reward in a career hampered by injuries. Bill made 282 appearances, scoring 4 times.

Roy Little joined City from Greenwood Victoria in August 1949. Cool under pressure and with good distribution skills, he was an important member of the City side that reached successive Cup Finals. Roy played 187 times at full-back for City, scoring just twice.

Les McDowell welcomes the Cup-holders back for pre-season training in July 1956, but unfortunately they would underachieve. The following season, 1957/58, however, would be a different story and notable because the players not only scored but also conceded a century of goals and finished an exciting season in fifth place. In a madcap campaign City dazzled Chelsea 5-2, Tottenham 5-1 and Everton 6-2, but collapsed at Preston 1-6, Leicester 4-8 and West Brom 2-9. As they say 'it's a funny old game'!

Three
Rockin' and Rollin' to the Top

NEWCASTLE UNITED FOOTBALL CLUB
ST. JAMES' PARK · NEWCASTLE
GROUND CAPACITY — 70,000
RECORD ATTENDANCE — 68,386

WE WELCOME TODAY —

Manchester City
Sat., 25th October, 1958 kick-off 3.0 p.m.

3D

OFFICIAL PROGRAMME

In 1958/59 the campaign would go down to the very last match before safety was achieved, City supporters having to be grateful for a last minute West Brom equaliser at Villa Park even though their own team had defeated Leicester 3-1. One of the twenty-two defeats during the campaign came at St James Park – note the ground capacity! City did get their revenge later in the season, winning 5-1.

LEEDS UNITED A.F.C.

PRO·REGE·ET·LEGE

SEASON
1958-1959

OFFICIAL PROGRAMME 3d.

City's best winning sequence in 1958/59 (three out of four games) came with victories over Leeds 4-0, Portsmouth 4-3 and Newcastle United 5-1, the latter two matches being their only consecutive wins of the season.

The 1960s were just weeks away when City had their biggest win of the 1959/60 season: 5-1 at Preston, with McAdams grabbing three of the goals. McAdams' hat-trick was one of three he struck during the campaign, but unusually his others had little effect as City lost to Wolves 4-6 and Newcastle 3-4. During this season the club broke the British transfer record by splashing out £55,000 on Denis Law, who in his first short spell at Maine Road would score six at Luton in the FA Cup, a match destined to be abandoned, with City losing the re-match 1-3.

The 1961/62 season was another mediocre one for City. The campaign did, however, see the debut of Glyn Pardoe, who at the age of 15 years 314 days became the club's youngest ever player.

MANCHESTER CITY
FOOTBALL CLUB LTD

SEASON 1960-61

COVERED ACCOMMODATION FOR 50,000

SATURDAY, 25th FEB., 1961   Kick-off 3.0 p.m.
TOTTENHAM HOTSPUR

Official Programme Fourpence

F.A. CUP WINNERS 1904, 1934, 1956   MANCHESTER CITY HONOURS LIST   LEAGUE CHAMPIONS 1937
FINALISTS 1926, 1933, 1955   RUNNERS-UP 1904, 1921

DIVISION II CHAMPIONS
1899, 1903, 1910, 1928, 1947
RUNNERS-UP 1896, 1951

City may have struggled, but (frustratingly) on their day they could beat the best, as illustrated by a 6-2 thrashing of current League Champions Tottenham Hotspur in March 1962.

The 1962/63 season was extended due to a horrendous winter. City began with a 1-8 defeat at Wolves and ended it with a 1-6 defeat at West Ham (one of six in their last eight games of the campaign). The latter result, however, was merely a statistic as relegation had already been confirmed in the previous match with a home defeat in the Manchester derby (a result City would avenge in 1974). However, although first team regulars Alan Oakes, Neil Young and newcomer Harry Dowd were not aware of it, the 1960s glory team was beginning to form. The team needed to be rebuilt, but not by Les McDowell, who after thirteen seasons was replaced by George Poyser in June 1963. Under McDowell City had won promotion to Division One and appeared in two FA Cup finals. An innovative manager, he will always be famous because of his association with the Revie plan.

Above: Manchester City FC, 1963/64. From left to right, back row: Meadows (trainer), Leivers, Wood, Sear, Dowd, Oakes, Wagstaffe, Betts. Front row: Kennedy, Panter, Grasy, Poyser (manager), Murray, Kevan, Young. Of Poyser's two seasons in charge, his first was by far the best as City finished sixth and goals flowed. Chief contributors were Kevan (30) and Murray (21), who during Christmas 1963 hit their richest vain of form against Rotherham (6-1) and Scunthorpe United (8-1 and 4-2), Murray grabbing 8 (including two hat-tricks) and Kevan 5. *Below*: One of many occasions when Kevan and Murray scored, this time a goal apiece at Gigg Lane on 28 December 1964.

BURY White Shirts Blue Shorts					Sky Blue Shirts White Shorts	MANCHESTER C.
		PILKINGTON 11	7 WAGSTAFFE	4 KENNEDY		
	LEECH 6					
CALLAGHER 3		BELL 10	8 GRAY		2 BACUZZI	
HARKER 1	BUNNER 5	YARD 9 ●	9 MURRAY	5 BATTY		1 DOWD
COLQUHOUN 2		GRIFFIN 8	10 KEVAN		3 SEAR	
	TURNER 4			6 OAKES		
		ALSTON 7	11 YOUNG			

Referee: J. PARKINSON (Blackburn).   Linesmen: G. E. Cartwright (Red Flag) and H. M. Jolly (Yellow Flag).

Pen Pictures of Today's Visitors

(Goal): Harry Dowd—A Manchester-born player who forged to the front after gaining experience in the junior ranks. Followed Bert Trautmann as first team goalkeeper, and quickly proved his worth despite his being rather on the small side. He makes up for this by his agility and remarkable sense of anticipation.

(Full Back): David Bacuzzi—Signed from Arsenal just before the end of the 1963-64 season, Bacuzzi is the son of former Fulham defender, Joe Bacuzzi. He began his career as an amateur with East-bourne, joined Arsenal in April, 1958, and turned professional a year later, making his debut in the Gunners' senior side in February, 1961. Made 46 League appearances for Arsenal, 22 of them in 1961-62 season. Born in London.

(Full Back): Cliff Sear—A native of Denbighshire, and a Welsh Under-23 and full International, Sear joined the City staff from Oswestry Town in 1957, made his League debut three months later, and has been a regular choice for most of the time ever since. A very solid and dependable player at all times.

(Wing-half or Full Back): Bob Kennedy—Capped as a wing-half by Scotland's Under-23 Selectors, Kennedy joined the Maine Road staff from Kilmarnock in the summer of 1961. Since his arrival has played in four full back positions, each of the wing-half berths, inside right and centre-forward.

(Wing- or Centre-half): Roy Cheetham—A native of Manchester, Cheetham has made his way to the top via the various junior sides, and the Central League team at Maine Road. Made his League debut in 1957-58 and has occupied several positions.

(Centre-half): Mike Batty—Manchester-born, Batty signed as a professional for City in July, 1961 after previous service as an amateur and apprentice professional. Made his debut for City in the First Division against Bolton Wanderers at Maine Road on April 13th, last year. Played his first senior game of this season at Middlesbrough on December 5th.

(Left-half): Alan Oakes—A former skipper of the Club's Youth side, Oakes signed his first professional form in 1959, making his League debut in November that year. Right from the start he showed ability beyond his years, and with the gradual gathering of experience has since developed into a very consistent player. Missed only one game last season.

(Outside-right): David Wagstaffe—Another local-born product of the City's junior sides, Wagstaffe made his League debut, as a teenager, in September, 1960. Very fast, with excellent ball-control and dribbling, he is a player of much promise who provides countless openings for his colleagues.

(Inside-forward or Wing-half): Matt Gray—Regarded as one of the best inside-forwards in Scotland when signed by the club in February, 1963 from Third Lanark, Gray has proved not only a good wing-half, but also a capable deputy goalkeeper. Finished last season at inside-right, after previously being at inside-right.

(Centre-forward): Jimmy Murray—Signed from Wolverhampton Wanderers on Guy Fawkes day last year, Murray soon gave a firework display, scoring no fewer than thirteen goals in his first eight league outings and fitting in splendidly with Kevan. Unfortunately an injury in a Cup-tie last season kept him aside for two months, but on returning he resumed where he had left off, finishing with 21 goals in 19 League outings.

(Inside-left): Derek Kevan—Previously with West Bromwich Albion and Chelsea, this former England international was signed by City in the summer of 1963 and finished a brilliant season with 30 goals in League games, being the first player to do so for City since Peter Doherty in 1936-37. Kevan had one fine run in which he scored 12 goals in eight consecutive matches in the League and League Cup. He has been capped by England on 14 occasions, in both inside-berths and also at centre-forward.

(Outside-left): Neil Young—Also a Mancunian by birth and a product of the junior sides, Young is another of the club's young players. His League debut was on November 25th, 1961, when 17, and he finished that season with 10 goals in 24 outings, a very good start. Can also play on the other flank, where he played most games last season, in which he missed only five matches.

(Centre-half): Alf Wood—Still another of the Club's own products, Wood was a member of the England Youth team last season and also had fifteen first-team outings in the Club's League and Cup matches. He made his senior debut in 1962-63, appearing in three matches. Considering his youth, did remarkably well last season.

(Inside-forward): Glyn Pardoe—Capped five times as a Schoolboy International, Pardoe became the youngest player ever to figure in the Club's League side when he made his debut on April 11th, 1962, against Birmingham City at Maine Road. He was then only 15 years and 314 days. He played in another three games that season, had four outings the following winter, and last season figured in twenty League matches, showing his versatility by appearing at inside-right, outside-right and centre-forward.

Records played on the ground kindly loaned by J. R. Calverley & Co. Ltd.

Manchester City FC, 1965/66. From left to right, back row: Mike Summerbee, Neil Young, Cliff Sear, Dave Bacuzzi, Mick Doyle, George Heslop, Alan Oakes. Fourth row: Malcolm Allison (assistant manager), Harry Dowd, Alan Ogley, Dave Ewing (assistant trainer). Third row: Johnny Hart (trainer), Bobby Kennedy, Glyn Pardoe, Peter Blakey (physiotherapist.). Second row: Dave Connor, Johnny Crossan (captain). Front row: Joe Mercer (manager). The start of Manchester City's most successful period began when Joe Mercer left his managerial post at Sheffield United to replace George Poyser in July 1965. His first appointment was an assistant...Malcolm Allison. In their first season under Mercer and Allison, City recorded their sixth Division Two title, yet no one could have predicted what success lay ahead. Mike Summerbee and George Heslop had arrived and immediately cemented their places in the first team, whilst a youngster called Colin Bell made his City debut. Skipper was skilful midfielder Johnny Crossan, who would stay for just two seasons, scoring 28 goals in his 110 appearances. It was during this season that Bobby Kennedy, who played at either wing-half or full-back, and stylish left-back Cliff Sear would both play their last games as regulars (251 and 279 appearances respectively), both having served the club loyally.

City lost just once in the opening fifteen fixtures of 1965/66, and of their seven victories the most emphatic was a 3-0 win at Deepdale, Neil Young scoring twice. Indeed, Young (14) would edge Crossan (13) in the goal-scoring stakes by the end of the season.

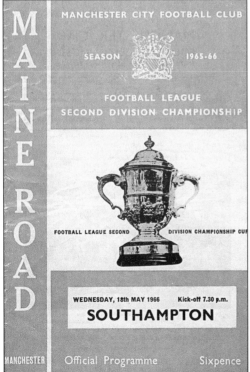

City's 5-0 win at home to Leyton Orient heralded a 22-match run that would see just one defeat and effectively clinch the title. With the title and promotion issues settled, City entertained runners-up Southampton for a party – the match ended 0-0!

Alan Oakes joined the club as an amateur in April 1958 and during eighteen seasons gave incredible service; although there may have been more flamboyant stars around, none were as consistent or as devoted. Oakes started out in a poor City side but went on to play his part in all the club's major honours of the 1960s and '70s. During his City career Alan won First and Second Division Championship medals, an FA Cup, a European Cup Winners Cup and two League Cup medals. Top of the all-time appearances list, Alan played a total of 676 (4) games, scoring 34 goals.

Neil Young started out as an apprentice professional at Maine Road before signing full-time in February 1961. Young always seemed to have something to spare, and is best remembered for his excellent ball control and shooting power. Top scorer in both City's Championship seasons of the 1960s, as well as First and Second Division Championship medals, Neil won European Cup Winners Cup and FA Cup winners medals. In all Young made a total of 413 (3) appearances for City, scoring 108 goals, none more memorable or important than his brace against Newcastle in the Championship decider in 1968, his winning strike in the '69 Cup Final, and his strike in the '70 Cup Winners Cup final.

Mick Doyle was one of the club's greatest players during the Mercer/Allison era. Starting out as a centre forward he made his name as a determined midfielder or defender, who was eventually appointed club captain. Mick won 5 caps for England and, along with Alan Oakes, is the only City player to win First and Second Division Championship, FA Cup, two League Cup, and European Cup Winners Cup winners medals. Third on the all-time appearances list, Mick played in 563 (7) matches, scoring 41 goals.

City's youngest debutante, Glyn Pardoe played in every position except goalkeeper and centre half during his fifteen seasons at the club. Glyn later returned as youth team coach. He won First and Second Division championship, FA Cup, League Cup and Cup Winners' Cup medals. In all he appeared 378 (2) times for City, scoring 23 goals, the most memorable being his winner in the 1970 League Cup final.

Mike Summerbee was Joe Mercer's first signing at Maine Road. Initially an orthodox outside-right, he created havoc for opposing defences with his accurate crossing. Summerbee eventually played a more versatile role and shared in many of the club's successes. A member of the First and Second Division Championship, FA Cup and 1970 League Cup winning sides, Mike is eighth on the all-time appearances list, having played a total of 449 (3) matches, scoring 68 goals. In addition, Mike was capped 8 times by England.

Colin Bell – nicknamed 'Nijinsky' because of his non-stop running, incredible stamina and boundless enthusiasm – is one of City's all-time greats. Signed from Bury in March 1966, after making his debut against City when only seventeen, Colin enjoyed tremendous success, winning First Division, FA Cup, League Cup and European Cup Winners Cup winners medals. Colin is fifth on the all-time appearances list, having played 498 (3) times for City, and third in the scoring charts with 153 goals – an amazing record (only Eric Brook comes close). These statistics would undoubtedly have been even better but for a serious knee injury in 1976 that forced him to retire in 1979.

Manchester City FC, 1966/67. From left to right, back row: Book, Pardoe, Kennedy, Sear, Heslop, Kennedy (physiotherapist). Middle row: Griffiths (secretary), Cheetham, Doyle, Horne, Dowd, Oakes, Summerbee, Allison (assistant manager) Front row: Bell, Young, Crossan (captain), Mercer (manager), Connor, Brand, Hart (trainer). Joe's 'boys of '66' are pictured here ready to tackle all-comers in Division One once again. In a season when the team would consolidate their status in the top-flight, Tony Book and Glyn Pardoe would win first team places. By 1967/68 only one piece of the Championship team was missing...Francis Lee. His arrival from Bolton for £60,000 in October 1967 would coincide with an unbeaten eleven-match run, yielding eight victories. In addition, Ken Mulhearn would briefly reign as City's number one 'keeper.

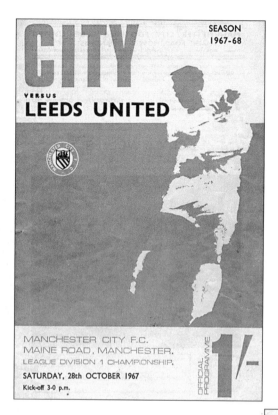

Match programme *v.* Leeds United, a game in which City gained a priceless 1-0 victory against one of the major contenders for the title with a Colin Bell strike.

During the vital Easter period City won both their home matches, against Chelsea 1-0 and West Ham 3-0. Even though Chelsea gained revenge at Stamford Bridge a few days later, City clinched their second Division One crown with victories in their final four matches against Sheffield Wednesday 1-0, Everton 2-0, Tottenham 3-1 and Newcastle United 4-3. This is the cover of the match programme from the Chelsea clash at Maine Road, where Mick Doyle's goal proved vital.

The Championship decider was played at Newcastle's St James Park ground, and what a thriller it was. This photograph shows Mike Summerbee scoring City's opener.

Francis Lee secures the title with City's fourth – before being mobbed!

It's over! City's final record for the season read: played 42, won 26, drawn 6 and lost 10; goals for 86 and goals against 43, with a total of 58 points. Top scorers were Young 19, Lee 16, Bell 14 and Summerbee 14. Whilst Tony Book played in all 42 League matches, a further five of the squad played in at least 40 of them.

Physiotherapist Peter Blakey pours champagne over skipper Book in the dressing room after the game. Looking on are Allison, Pardoe, Heslop, Young, Doyle, Mulhearn and Bell.

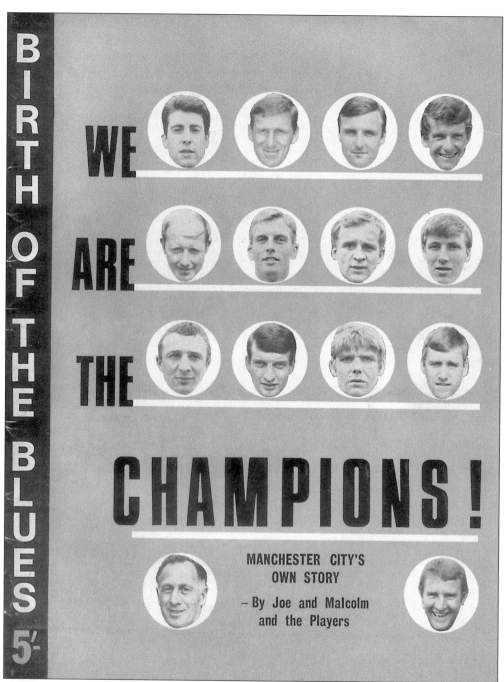

The Football League Champions.

Yet more silverware came to the club in August 1969 as City thrashed FA Cup winners West Brom 6-1 in the seasonal curtain raiser, the Charity Shield. The goals were split between Lee (2), Owen (2) and Young, the sixth coming from an own-goal. City were forced into a number of changes, the team being: Mulhearn, Connor, Pardoe, Doyle, Heslop, Oakes, Lee, Bell, Summerbee, Owen, Young.

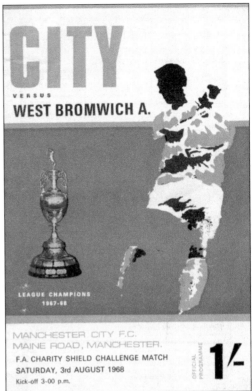

CITY
VERSUS
WEST BROMWICH A.

LEAGUE CHAMPIONS
1967-68

MANCHESTER CITY F.C.
MAINE ROAD, MANCHESTER.
F.A. CHARITY SHIELD CHALLENGE MATCH
SATURDAY, 3rd AUGUST 1968
Kick-off 3-00 p.m.

OFFICIAL PROGRAMME

1/-

Four lucky supporters, being supervised by Bell, show off the Charity Shield.

Manchester City FC, 1968/69. From left to right, back row: Oakes, Young, Heslop, Mulhearn, Bell, Pardoe, Summerbee. Front row: Allison (assistant manager), Connor, Lee, Book, Colman, Doyle, Hart (trainer). City's defence of the title never really got going – only seven wins by the turn of the year saw to that – however, they did have the satisfaction of being just one of two teams to claim the prize scalp of Champions-elect Leeds United, beating the Yorkshire side 3-1. They also played in the European Cup for the first time, but fell at the first hurdle to Hungarian side Fenerbahce.

As the season developed priorities soon switched as City made progress in the FA Cup, disposing of Luton 1-0 in the third round on 4 January 1969. This shot shows Lee in the thick of the action against the Hatters.

In the fourth round City overcame Newcastle United 2-0 in a replay at Maine Road in front of 60,844 spectators. *Above*: Owen scores the first. *Below*: Young settles the tie with the second goal.

A comfortable fifth round win at Blackburn set up a clash with Tottenham at Maine Road. Over 48,000 spectators witnessed a cracking match that was settled by a single Lee strike. *Above*: Lee strikes one of his two goals at Ewood Park. *Below*: Although Lee himself is out of shot, this is his winner against Tottenham in the quarter-finals.

Tommy Booth's last-minute goal in the semi-final against Everton took City back to Wembley for the first time in thirteen seasons. This photograph shows City displaying their Cup Final strip. From left to right, back row: Blakey (physiotherapist), Pardoe, Doyle, Oakes, Dowd, Bell, Booth, Ewing (trainer). Front row: Owen, Connor, Summerbee, Book (captain), Lee, Young, Coleman.

An FA Cup final brochure – one of many souvenirs from the big day. City lined up at Wembley as follows: Dowd, Book (captain), Pardoe, Doyle, Booth, Oakes, Summerbee, Bell, Lee, Young and Connor.

Maine Road to Wembley!

F.A. CUP FINAL. 1969
Manchester City Players'
Official Souvenir

2/6

Manchester City *v*. Leicester City FA Cup final programme and rosette. The game was played on 26 April 1969.

Despite failing to deliver their pre-match forecast of flowing football, City did more than enough to win the final. A single goal proved decisive, the strike being set up by Mike Summerbee with Neil Young clinically finishing. Here, Leicester's Peter Shilton dives in vain as Young strikes the only goal of the match.

We've won the Cup! From left to right: Pardoe, Lee, Young (background), Doyle, Dowd, Bell and Oakes. City's triumph enabled Mercer to join Wilf Wild as the only City manager to win both the League Championship and the FA Cup. After the match Young said of his winning goal: 'In these situations you don't have time to aim for a particular spot. You just sense the chance, hit it and hope for the best'.

Oakes and Dowd show off the trophy to delighted supporters. For 'keeper Dowd this would be his last big match. Within a season he would depart after 219 appearances and one goal (*v.* Bury in 1964).

A jubilant set of players during the victory parade in Manchester.

Above: Manchester City FC, 1969/70: From left to right, back row: Allison (assistant manager), unknown, Bowles, Owen, Booth, Young, Pardoe, Mulhearn, Dowd, Corrigan, Lee, Coleman, Summerbee, Doyle, Bell. Oakes, Heslop. Middle row: Mercer (manager), Blakey (physiotherapist), Donachie, Bowyer, Glennon, Towers, Cunliffe, Jackson, Jeffries, Howell, Mundy, Connor, Book, Ewing (trainer), Godwin (chief scout). Front row: Hart (youth manager), Keegan, Hatton, Curtin, Lukes, Brennan, Healey, Clarke, Milner, Curtin. In a remarkable season, though City would finish mid-table, they would not only complete their domination of cup competitions but also claim a United treble during the five clashes between the rivals in the campaign. *Below*: The first victory over United was a League encounter at Maine Road, Bell pictured here scoring one of his brace of goals in the 4-0 rout. City completed the League double with a 2-1 win at Old Trafford.

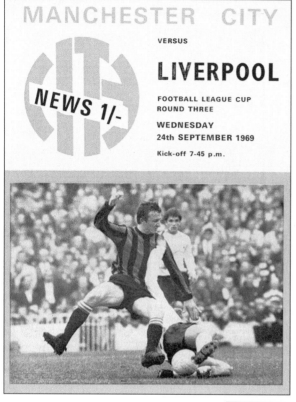

Wembley was once again on the supporters' minds following victories over Southport 3-0, Liverpool 3-2, Everton 2-0 and QPR 3-0 in the League Cup. This is the match programme from the clash with Liverpool in the third round.

The programme from the fourth round encounter with Everton.

In a season when all 92 League clubs entered the competition for the first time, one team stood in City's way of a place in the League Cup final ... Manchester United. The semi-final clashes were classics. City won the home leg 2-1 thanks to goals by Bell and Lee, before putting in an exceptional performance in the return, drawing 2-2 for a 4-3 aggregate win. This is a match ticket from the clash at Old Trafford, in which Summerbee and Bowyer scored the vital goals.

MANCHESTER UTD. F.C. LTD.
OLD TRAFFORD, MANCHESTER

LEAGUE CUP
SEMI-FINAL — Second Leg

MANCHESTER UTD.
v
MANCHESTER CITY

Wednesday, 17th December
Kick-off 7-45 p.m.

Admission 12/-

L. Olive
Secretary.

STAND
E

UNRESERVED SEAT

ADULTS

Enter by Turnstiles
50, 57—58

No   982

Issued subject to the Rules, Regulations and
Bye-Laws of the Football Association.
No Ticket exchanged nor money refunded.

This Portion to be Retained

As a capacity attendance is expected, it is strongly recommended that patrons ENTER THE GROUND not less than 30 minutes before kick-off.

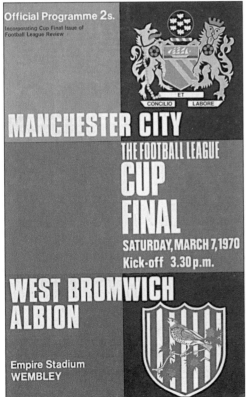

The League Cup final was against West Brom and played at Wembley on 7 March 1970.

87

Tony Book introduces Sir Stanley Rous to the team during the pre-match formalities, before wishing West Brom skipper Doug Fraser the best of luck before kick-off. City's line-up for this occasion was: Corrigan, Book (captain), Mann, Doyle, Booth, Oakes, Summerbee (Bowyer), Bell, Lee, Heslop and Pardoe.

In a thrilling final, played on a quagmire of a pitch, Mick Doyle cancelled out Jeff Astle's sixth-minute opener, but the only real surprise was that City, who created many chances, had to go into extra-time before claiming victory through Glyn Pardoe's first goal of the season. These two photographs show substitute Ian Bowyer, and the City bench, simultaneously celebrating Pardoe's defining moment of the match.

Another trophy… another lap of honour. *Above*: Goalscorers Doyle and Pardoe celebrate as the team complete their sweep of domestic honours in three seasons. *Left*: Bell and Oakes join the goalscorers. After the match Joe Mercer was delighted and said: 'What a magnificent side. I was worried when Albion went ahead because Joe Corrigan should have got that ball, but we made up for it afterwards, and as for Tony Book, what a great captain…what a great man'. Francis Lee was undoubtedly Man of the Match and explained that: 'Everything I tried came off, that's why I told Malcolm before extra-time to tell the lads to let me have as much of the ball as they could'.

FA Cup success the previous season meant European Cup Winners Cup football and City faced Atletico Bilbao. This is the match programme from the second leg clash, following a thrilling 3-3 draw in the opening game.

Bowyer scores the crucial opening goal against Bilbao at Maine Road. The match ended 3-0 to City (6-3 on aggregate).

In the second round City travelled to Norway for the opening leg with part-timers SK Lierse. Unsurprisingly, City comfortably qualified with an aggregate 8-0 victory. Francis Lee is shown scoring one of his brace of goals in Lierse; the game finished 3-0.

MANCHESTER CITY

NEWS 1/-

VERSUS

ACADEMICA DE COIMBRA

EUROPEAN CUP WINNERS' CUP

4th Finals — 2nd Leg

WEDNESDAY

18th MARCH 1970

Kick-off 7-30 p.m.

City played their quarter-final first leg against Academica Coimbra on the Wednesday before the League Cup final, and in the circumstances excelled themselves. The opening tie with Coimbra was a tight affair, with City delighted to take a 0-0 draw back to Manchester. This is the match programme for the return leg, four days after City's Wembley win.

The return with Coimbra remained scoreless throughout the ninety minutes. *Above*: Malcolm Allison gives the players some words of wisdom before the extra-time period. It did the trick as City went through to the semi-finals in sensational fashion, substitute Tony Towers scoring the only goal in the last minute of the match. *Below*: City players turn in triumph after Towers' late strike.

In the semi-finals against German side Schalke 04, the players overturned a first-leg deficit to comfortably reach their first European final. Here, Lee goes close with a header. He later made up for this miss by scoring one of City's five goals in the 5-2 aggregate win.

29. APRIL 1970
EUROPACUP-FINALSPIEL
DER POKALSIEGER

MANCHESTER CITY – GORNIK-ZABRZE

HERAUSGEGEBEN
VOM ÖSTERREICHISCHEN FUSSBALL-BUND
IM AUFTRAG DER U. E. F. A.

The match programme (Polish version) for the European Cup Winners Cup final between Manchester City and Gornik Zabrzeon 29 April 1970. City's line-up for this historic match was as follows: Corrigan, Book (captain), Pardoe, Doyle, Booth, Oakes, Heslop, Bell, Lee, Young, Towers.

Neil Young bundles home City's opening goal on a rain-soaked evening in Vienna, where a crowd of just 10,000 witnessed the club's greatest European night as Gornik Zabrze were defeated 2-1.

Francis Lee turns away after slotting home the penalty that proved to be the winning goal.

Soaking wet but clearly happy at the end of the match are this delighted trio of Booth, Bowyer (who replaced the injured Doyle) and Heslop. This would be Heslop's last big match for the club. A reliable understudy in his latter years, he rarely let the team down during 195 (3) appearances. Apart from being a member of the Cup Winners Cup team he had also played in City's League Cup winning side a few weeks earlier and both of City's Championship squads of the 1960s.

Tony Book raises his fourth trophy in three seasons. City now had the honour of becoming the first English side to win a European competition and all three domestic trophies.

Not a player in sight, but the European Cup Winners Cup sits proudly in the airport lounge at Vienna Airport – complete with a trilby!

Francis Lee acts as cheerleader on the steps of Manchester Town Hall as Malcolm Allison shows the trophy to fans. Tony Book and Mike Summerbee are also in the picture.

Tony Book made his top-flight debut at thirty-one. One of the best and quickest defenders seen at Maine Road, Tony was an inspirational skipper and captained the team throughout their glory years, collecting the Division One, FA Cup, League Cup and European Cup Winners Cup trophies. Voted joint Footballer of the Year in 1969 with Dave Mackay, Tony played 312 (3) games for City, scoring 5 times. He later went on to manage the club, guiding them to the League Cup in 1976.

Francis Lee joined from Bolton Wanderers and soon became a firm favourite with fans. Though not tall, his solid physique and bustling style made him a handful for defences and his thundering shot brought him lots of goals. An expert penalty taker, he struck a club-record 15 in 1971/72. He won a host of honours with City, playing in the victorious Division One, FA Cup, League Cup and European Cup Winners Cup sides, as well as representing England on 27 occasions. In February 1994 he became chairman before resigning during the 1997/98 season. In all, Lee made 328 (2) appearances for the club, scoring 148 goals.

Tommy Booth broke into the first team in October '68 and went on to become City's first choice centre half for a number of years (though at times he also played midfield when required), gaining winners medals in the FA Cup, League Cup, and European Cup Winners Cup. Seventh on the all-time appearances list, Tommy played a total of 487 (4) matches for City, scoring 37 goals, the most important being the FA Cup semi-final winner against Everton in 1969.

Joe Corrigan joined City as a junior in 1966 and went on to maintain City's tradition of producing fine goalkeepers. After initially replacing Dowd and Mulhearn, Joe overcame the loss of his place to Keith McRae in 1974 to become City's longest serving custodian. Second on the all-time appearances list, he is one of just two players to have broken the magical 600 barrier. In all, Joe appeared 602 (1) times for City, winning a European Cup Winners Cup and two League Cup winners medals. Joe also won 9 England caps.

In 1970/71 City had their best start to a top-flight campaign for sixty-six years, but couldn't maintain their form, eventually finishing eleventh. Off the field, Joe Mercer became general manager, with Malcolm Allison taking over first-team affairs. This is the double Cup winners line-up prior to the start of the season.

City got off to a shaky start in their defence of the Cup Winners Cup, and only just avoided going out at the first stage to part-timers Linfield, but squeezed through on away goals. There were no such problems in the next round though as they overcame Honved 3-0 on aggregate. This is action from the first leg in Budapest, where City won with a Colin Bell goal.

In the quarter-finals City were drawn to face Gornik Zabrze. Their opponents were out for revenge after their defeat the previous season, and looked odds-on after taking a 2-0 lead in the first leg. However, City's never-say-die attitude enabled them to square the aggregate scores by the end of the return, Mellor and Doyle scoring. To decide the tie, UEFA ordered a play-off in Copenhagen. *Above*: Lee celebrates scoring City's second in a brilliant 3-1 win. *Below*: Scorers Booth, Lee and Young toast their success as they await Chelsea in the semi-finals. Sadly, two 1-0 defeats by the Stamford Bridge side meant that their defence of the trophy was over.

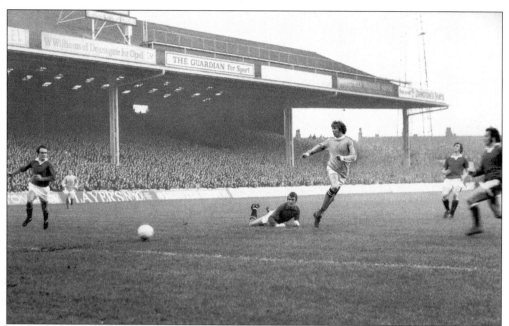

In 1971/72 City again won the Charity Shield, defeating Aston Villa 1-0. They should also have won their third League Championship, but Malcolm Allison's controversial signing of Rodney Marsh backfired as the team gained just ten points from their last nine matches, leaving them one point short. Arguably the most entertaining match of the season was their 3-3 draw with United. This is Bell calmly slotting home Lee's pinpoint cross for City's second in the Manchester derby on 6 November 1971.

In 1971/72 Francis Lee had his most productive season in a City shirt, scoring 35 goals in all competitions. Here, he back-heads his 31st goal of the campaign in a 3-1 win at Old Trafford.

Four
Blood, Sweat and Tears

At the end of the 1971/72 season, Joe Mercer left Maine Road to become general manager at Coventry City, before taking temporary charge of England in 1977. An all-time great both as a player and manager, Joe restored pride back in the club whilst guiding them to a host of honours. Without doubt the most successful manager in City's history, his successor Malcolm Allison would last just a few months before being replaced by Johnny Hart in March 1973. Sadly, due to ill health, Hart's tenure was cut short and Ron Saunders took over in November 1973. Still leading the line was the attacking trio of Bell, Lee and Summerbee. Has their ever been a greater strike-force at the club?

Manchester City FC, 1973/74. From left to right, back row: Barrett, Doyle, Booth, Pardoe. Middle row: Book (assistant manager), Donachie, Carrodus, Macrae, Corrigan, Oakes, Leman, Allcock (coach). Front row: Law, Lee, Summerbee, Saunders (manager), Bell, Marsh, Towers.

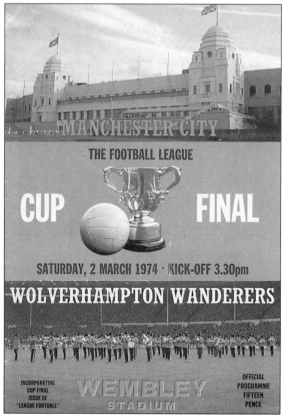

Four seasons after triumphing in the League Cup, City reached Wembley again. You could argue they had a charmed draw, facing just one Division One side – but the supporters weren't complaining. Victories over Walsall 4-0 (after two 0-0 draws), Carlisle 1-0, York City 4-1 (after a replay), Coventry 4-2 (after a 2-2 draw) and Plymouth Argyle 3-1 on aggregate, pitched them against a much-fancied Wolves team in the final. This is the match programme from Wembley, where City lined up with a rich array of talent: McRae, Pardoe, Donachie, Doyle, Booth, Towers, Summerbee, Bell, Lee, Law and Marsh.

Sadly, the only bright moment for City supporters at Wembley was this Colin Bell strike.

Summerbee and Lee manage to raise a smile during the walk back to the dressing rooms after the 2-1 defeat, but for everyone at the club it was a bitterly disappointing result. Saunders was dismissed in the aftermath of the defeat, his assistant Tony Book bringing some much-needed stability to the club. Both Summerbee and Lee would depart Maine Road within twelve months as Book started the unenviable task of replacing many of the players he had captained during the glory years.

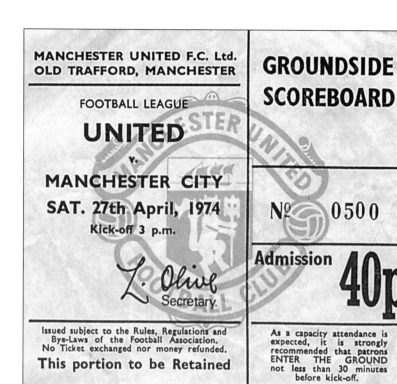

MANCHESTER UNITED F.C. Ltd.
OLD TRAFFORD, MANCHESTER

FOOTBALL LEAGUE

UNITED
v.
MANCHESTER CITY
SAT. 27th April, 1974
Kick-off 3 p.m.

L. Olive
Secretary.

Issued subject to the Rules, Regulations and
Bye-Laws of the Football Association.
No Ticket exchanged nor money refunded.

This portion to be Retained

GROUNDSIDE
SCOREBOARD

Nº 0500

Admission 40p

As a capacity attendance is
expected, it is strongly
recommended that patrons
ENTER THE GROUND
not less than 30 minutes
before kick-off.

Although the 1973/74 League campaign was far from a vintage City performance, fans will always remember one match in particular – the day skipper-for-the-day Denis Law relegated his beloved Manchester United to Division Two. This is a match ticket from this significant match.

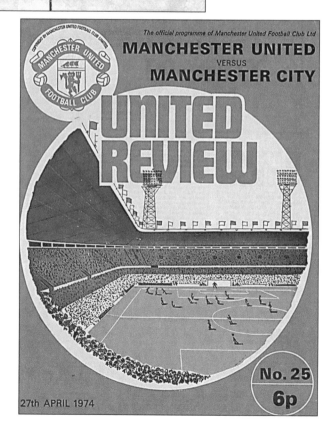

The programme for the extraordinary Manchester United *v.* Manchester City fixture, 27 April 1974.

The official programme of Manchester United Football Club Ltd

MANCHESTER UNITED
VERSUS
MANCHESTER CITY

UNITED
REVIEW

No. 25
6p

27th APRIL 1974

For Dennis this brilliant piece of opportunism was pure heartache – and there was no trademark celebration afterwards.

The match was abandoned shortly after the goal when fans invaded the pitch. The result stood...United were down. United fans wishing to console him mobbed the distraught Dennis Law.

In 1974/75 City finished eighth, a feat they repeated twelve months later. In addition they delighted supporters by once again reaching the League Cup final…and in some style. Their run to Wembley had taken place mainly at Maine Road, but nobody could dispute their endeavour following victories over Norwich 6-1 (after 1-1 and 2-2 draws); Nottingham Forest 2-1; Manchester United (now back in the top-flight) 4-0; Mansfield 4-2 and Middlesborough in the semi-finals 4-1 on aggregate. In the final they faced Newcastle United and 'SuperMac' Malcolm Macdonald. *Above:* City's 1975/76 squad. *Below:* Since signing for City, Dennis Tueart had become a real favourite with fans and is pictured here striking after just 38 seconds in the fourth round clash with United.

Manchester City *v.* Middlesborough, League Cup semi-final second leg.

Just look at those flares! The team pose in their Wembley suits prior to setting off for Wembley. At the helm is new boss Tony Book.

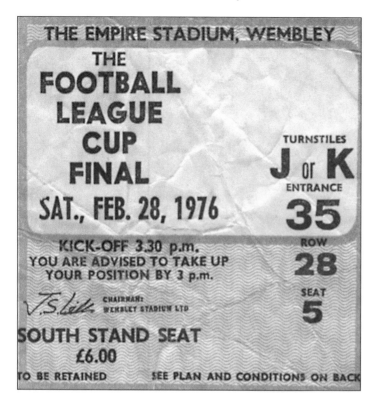

The match ticket for Manchester City *v.* Newcastle United, 28 February 1976.

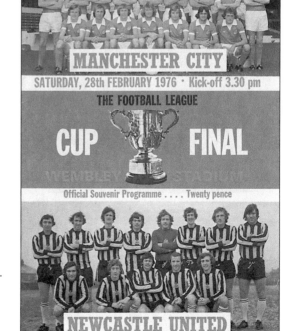

The programme for the League Cup final. City lined up as follows: Corrigan, Keegan, Donachie, Doyle (captain), Watson, Oakes, Barnes, Booth, Royle, Hartford, Tueart.

City's Doyle and Watson snuff out any danger posed by 'Supermac'.

It's celebration time after Dennis Tueart's amazing over-head kick won the League Cup for City. Here, he receives a hug from Tommy Booth and Asa Hartford.

It's ours again…skipper Doyle lifts the League Cup! After three Wembley wins in seven seasons, supporters would have to wait an unbelieveable twenty-three years to see another winning City team at the twin-towers.

Helen Turner, one of City's most extrovert supporters, joins the players during the lap of honour.

All smiles as City show-off the League Cup.

Two of the Wembley heroes, Mick Doyle and Joe Corrigan, share a joke on the open-top bus during the victory parade through Manchester city centre.

Willie Donachie joined City as a junior in 1968. This classy defender became a full international for Scotland before he was twenty-two, eventually winning 35 caps. One of the best defenders of his era, Willie was a member of City's 1976 League Cup winning side. Tenth on the all-time list for appearances, he played a total of 431(5) games, scoring just twice. He still has an active role at Maine Road as assistant manager to Joe Royle.

Dennis Tueart joined City from Sunderland for £275,000 in March 1974. One of the best forwards of his generation, he excited crowds wherever he played. City fans will always remember Dennis for his spectacular overhead-kick that won the League Cup in 1976. One of only fourteen players to have scored a century of goals for the club, Dennis played a total of 265 (10) matches for City, scoring 109 times. He also represented England on 6 occasions. Currently is still at City as a director of the club.

Asa Hartford hit the headlines in 1971 when his proposed transfer to Leeds United fell through when what seemed a routine medical spotted a 'hole in the heart'. However, the condition proved to be minor and he joined City from West Brom for £250,000 in August 1974. His stamina and forceful play delighted supporters, and he went on to gain 36 caps for Scotland – more than any other City player. A key member of the team during his time at the club, Asa made 320 (1) appearances and scored 36 goals. Currently he is reserve team manager at Maine Road.

Dave Watson followed Dennis Tueart to Maine Road in June 1975. A no-nonsense centre half, he quickly cemented his place in the side, eventually captaining the team. Acknowledged as one of the most reliable defenders of his era, Watson made a total of 188 appearances for City, scoring 6 times, before moving to Werder Bremen in 1979. In addition he represented England on 65 occasions, scoring 4 goals.

Joe Royle was born in Liverpool and, after a making his name at Everton, joined City in 1974 for £170,000. His three seasons at Maine Road proved successful, Joe adding a League Cup winners medal to his League Championship medal gained at Everton. A little unfortunate to win just 6 England caps, his all-action style leading the line made him a handful for defences and a favourite with supporters. During his spell at City, Joe made 122 (2) appearances, scoring 31 times. In February 1998 he took over as manager at Maine Road, guiding them to the Premier League after consecutive promotion seasons.

Before signing as a professional in July 1975, Paul Power combined studying at Leeds Polytechnic with playing reserve team football for City. He went on to experience the euphoria of relegation and promotion with City. Operating on the left flank in either defence or midfield, Paul was handed the captaincy in 1979 by Malcolm Allison, skippering the side to the 1981 FA Cup and 1986 Full Members Cup finals. During fourteen seasons Paul made a total of 436 (9) appearances for City, placing him ninth on the all-time list, and scored 36 goals – the most memorable being his semi-final winner against Ipswich Town in 1981. Today he is part of the club's academy coaching staff.

In 1976/77, City at last found consistency throughout a campaign. They actually lost fewer games than in the 1968 Championship season, but unfortunately fourteen draws cost them dear, Liverpool pinching the title by a point. *Above*: City's 1976/77 squad. *Below*: The team depart for a pre-season tour of Spain.

FIRST DIVISION   v TOTTENHAM HOTSPUR

SATURDAY MAY 7th 1977 K.O. 3.00 pm

PRICE 15pence

Top scorers in 1976/77 were Brian Kidd (21) and Dennis Tueart (18), the highlights of the campaign being 5-0 thrashings dished out to Leicester City (new-boy Kidd becoming the first City player to score four goals in a League match since 1939) and Tottenham.

City were also back in Europe, and in the UEFA Cup they drew a glamour tie first round against Italian giants Juventus.

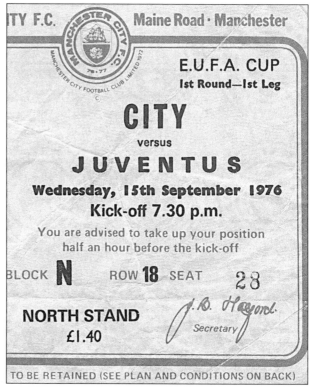

...ITY F.C.   Maine Road · Manchester

E.U.F.A. CUP
1st Round—1st Leg

CITY

versus

JUVENTUS

Wednesday, 15th September 1976

Kick-off 7.30 p.m.

You are advised to take up your position half an hour before the kick-off

BLOCK N   ROW 18   SEAT   28

NORTH STAND
£1.40

Secretary

TO BE RETAINED (SEE PLAN AND CONDITIONS ON BACK)

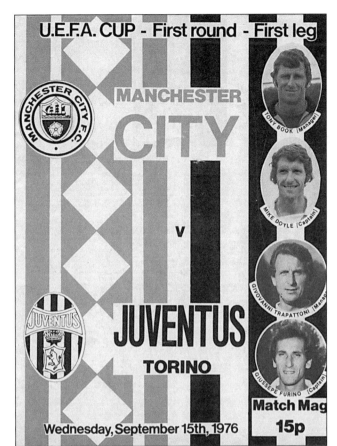

Right: The match programme from the Juve clash. *Below*: Mick Doyle and the Juventus defenders watch anxiously as Kidd's header finds the net. Sadly, City lost the return leg 2-0.

Domestically, the 1977/78 season was a disappointment. Though they finished fourth, consistency cost City dear as they mixed winning streaks with (numerous) off-days. They reached the quarter-finals of the League Cup before falling to Arsenal, and embarrassingly lost to Shrewsbury in the FA Cup. Again Kidd top-scored in the League, however Tueart grabbed the headlines, scoring hat-tricks against Aston Villa, Chelsea and Newcastle. One of City's best displays was a 3-1 win over United, Kidd scoring twice against his former club. The other scorer, Mick Channon, is seen above after finding the net in the United clash, whilst below he glides home City's second against Widzew Lodz. Agonisingly, City went out of the UEFA Cup on away goals after drawing 2-2 in the first leg at Maine Road.

Manchester City FC, 1978/79. From left to right, back row: Palmer, Futcher, Booth, Corrigan, Clements, Bell, Bennett. Middle row: Book (manager), Bailey, Power, Henry, Donachie, Ranson, Coughlin, Taylor. Front row: Owen, Barnes, Kidd, Watson, Hartford, Channon, Keegan. A decade on from their FA Cup triumph, the campaign would end with just Tommy Booth still in the side, Colin Bell finally retiring after his four-year battle against injury.

City slumped to fifteenth in Division One, but got off to a more encouraging start in the UEFA Cup when they drew 1-1 against Twente Enschede. Here, Peter Barnes hurdles past the outstretched leg of Twente defender Niels Overweg to set up a City attack in the first leg. Barnes, who won full England honours, was one of father Ken's two sons to represent City, but never quite reached the potential his early performances promised. He eventually made 149 appearances for City, scoring 22 goals.

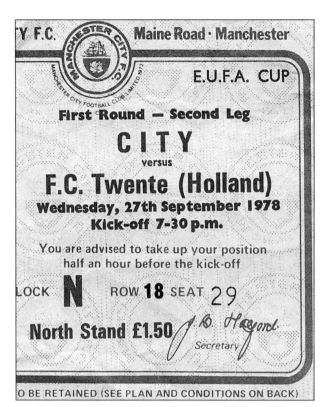

In the second leg City squeezed past Twente Enschede 3-2 to win 4-3 on aggregate.

A powerful 4-0 win over Standard Liege in the second round set up what should have been a straightforward return leg, but in a fiery match City lost 2-0 and had Gary Owen sent off. Their reward for the aggregate win was another glamour tie, this time against AC Milan.

At Milan's San Siro stadium City put on one of their best-ever European displays as they held their illustrious opponents to a 2-2 draw. Here, the skippers exchange pennants before the match.

City's goalscorers in Italy were Power and Kidd. In this photograph, three Milan defenders watch helplessly as Power scores his side's opening goal.

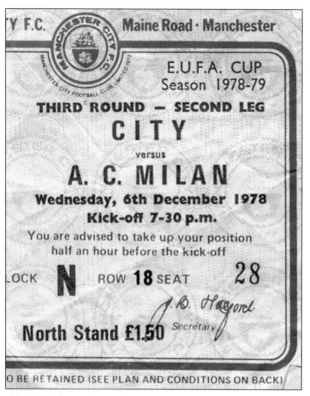

A ticket and programme from City's clash with Milan on 6 December 1978.

At Maine Road, City gained a resounding 3-0 win to complete a tremendous 5-2 aggregate triumph. *Above*: Hartford thumps home an unstoppable shot for the second goal. *Below*: Hartford enjoys a celebratory drink with the other scorers on the night, Kidd and Booth. During his near-three seasons at Maine Road, Kidd vindicated City's somewhat controversial decision to sign him from their neighbours at Old Trafford, in all scoring 57 goals in his 127 appearances for the club. Following spells at Arsenal and Everton, Kidd is amongst a small group of players to have played in a Manchester, North London and Merseyside derby.

E.U.F.A. CUP QUARTER FINAL — 1st LEG

TY F.C. Maine Road · Manchester

Manchester City

versus

Borussia Moenchengladbach

Wednesday, 7th March 1979
Kick-off 7-30 p.m.

You are advised to take up your position
half an hour before the kick-off

LOCK **N** ROW **18** SEAT **28**

Secretary

North Stand £1.60

TO BE RETAINED (SEE PLAN AND CONDITIONS ON BACK)

Sadly, City's UEFA Cup run would end in the fourth round when Borussia Monchengladbach triumphed on aggregate 4-2. To date this is City's last European venture. The 1979/80 pre-season saw Tony Book move internally to become general manager, with Malcolm Allison returning to first-team duties. The new manager's imports included Kaziniera Deyna, Dragoslav Stepanovic, and – record signing at nearly £1.5 million – Steve Daley. All of these players failed to settle.

City started the 1970s chasing silverware both at home and abroad. A decade later they suffered the humiliation of being knocked out of the FA Cup by Halifax Town. Their League campaign also ended frustratingly with the team slipping to seventeenth in the table. The 1980s could hardly have started on a more disappointing note, and Malcolm Allison's tenure was nearly over.

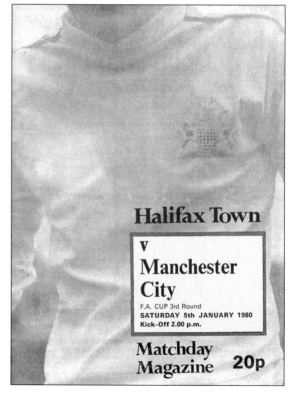

Halifax Town

v

Manchester City

F.A. CUP 3rd Round
SATURDAY 5th JANUARY 1980
Kick-Off 2.00 p.m.

Matchday Magazine 20p

When City opened the 1980/81 campaign without a win in twelve games, the inevitable managerial change followed with the appointment of John Bond. A season after the Halifax debacle, City confounded their critics by reaching Wembley again. Amazingly, this was the first time they had progressed beyond the fifth round since winning the FA Cup in 1969. Their run accounted for Crystal Palace 4-0, Norwich City 6-0, Peterborough 1-0, Everton 3-1 (after a 2-2 draw) and the highly-fancied Ipswich Town 1-0. *Right*: The match programme from the semi-final clash with Ipswich, where a cracking Paul Power free kick sent City to Wembley. *Below*: City's Cup Final squad. From left to right, back row: Reid, Booth, Hutchison, Corrigan, Caton, Henry, McDonald. Front row: Bowyer, Tueart, Ranson, Reeves, Power (captain), Bennett, Gow, Mackenzie.

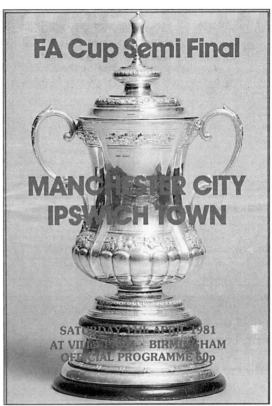

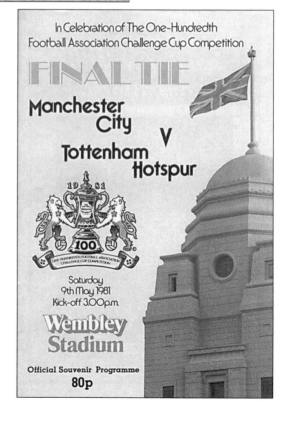

THE EMPIRE STADIUM, WEMBLEY

No ticket genuine unless it carries
a Lion's Head watermark below

19 81

100

ONE HUNDREDTH FOOTBALL ASSOCIATION
CHALLENGE CUP COMPETITION

FINAL TIE
SATURDAY, MAY, 9 1981
KICK-OFF 3.00 p.m.
YOU ARE ADVISED TO TAKE UP
YOUR POSITION BY 2.30 p.m.
1. This ticket is not transferable.
2. This counterfoil must be re-
tained for at least 6 months.

J.S.Lett CHAIRMAN:
WEMBLEY STADIUM LTD

NORTH TERRACE SEAT
£11.00

TO BE RETAINED   SEE PLAN AND CONDITIONS ON BACK

TURNSTILES

E

ENTRANCE
4
ROW
15
SEAT
290

A ticket for the 1981
FA Cup final.

In Celebration of The One-Hundredth
Football Association Challenge Cup Competition

FINAL TIE

Manchester
City   v
Tottenham
Hotspur

19 81

100

ONE HUNDREDTH FOOTBALL ASSOCIATION
CHALLENGE CUP COMPETITION

Saturday
9th May 1981
Kick-off 3.00p.m.

Wembley
Stadium

Official Souvenir Programme
80p

The match programme for the 1981 FA
Cup final between Tottenham and
Manchester City. City lined up as follows:
Corrigan, Ranson, McDonald, Reid,
Power, Caton, Bennett (Henry), Gow,
Mackenzie, Hutchison, Reeves.

To say Tommy Hutchison had mixed emotions after the drawn final is an understatement. *Above*: He watches in horror after deflecting Glen Hoddle's free kick past Joe Corrigan to give Tottenham the lead. *Below*: Hutchinson lies underneath a happy bunch of City players after scoring the equaliser.

Match ticket for the 1981 FA Cup final replay. City's side in the replay differed only in terms of the substitute, Tueart replacing Henry.

Match programme for the 1981 FA Cup final replay.

In the second game, Tottenham struck first through Ricki Villa before a Steve Mackenzie scorcher and Kevin Reeves penalty gave City the lead early in the second half. Unfortunately, a late strike from Garth Crooks sent the match into extra-time before Villa capped a remarkable personal performance with a memorable solo effort. Though defeated, City had been part of a final still regarded as the greatest since the 1953 'Matthews' final. *Above*: Reeves makes no mistake from the spot. *Below*: A couple of second later and Reeves celebrates as Power races to congratulate him. Reeves went on to score 39 goals for City in his 157 (1) appearances.

Manchester City FC, 1981/82. From left to right, back row: Pardoe (reserve team manager), Sainty (chief coach), Hutchison, Hareide, Bond, Booth, Williams, Corrigan, Caton, O'Neil, McDonald, Ranson, Benson, (assistant manager), Bond (manager). Front row: Bailey (trainer), Francis, Gow, Reid, Power, Reeves, Bennett, Tueart, Bowyer, Scott (youth coach). Bond's new-look side included £1.2 million signing Trevor Francis, but there was no longer a place for Tommy Booth; this severed all links with the glory side. City finished tenth, which was their highest placing in four seasons, but sadly it was a false dawn. Bond resigned in February 1983 after a humiliating 0-4 defeat in the FA Cup at Brighton. John Benson replaced him, but worse was to come. Having sat safely in ninth place when Bond departed, City won just four of their remaining seventeen games; relegation would come in the last game at home to Luton, when a draw would have sent the Hatters down. Unfortunately, City's opponents achieved safety through Radi Antic's late winner, which relegated City instead.

Five

Yo-Yo Years

Initially life in Division Two under new boss Billy McNeil seemed a breeze as City won eleven of their opening fifteen fixtures, but as the season progressed performances dipped and they had to settle for fourth place – one position off promotion. The campaign also saw defenders Ray Ranson and Tommy Caton play their final games for City after 233 and 197 appearances respectively, both having served the club loyally. Twelve months later, after a slow start, performances had picked up, and despite the odd hiccup they eventually claimed the third promotion spot on the last day of the campaign, defeating Charlton 5-1 in front of on an ecstatic home crowd. This is the match programme from the promotion clincher.

City struggled in 1985/86, winning just eleven games, and but for five straight wins in the opening weeks of '86 they would have been relegated. There was, however, the consolation of winning the FA Youth Cup for the first time, with a 3-1 aggregate victory over United, and an appearance at Wembley in the Full Members Cup final after defeating Leeds, Sheffield United, Sunderland and Hull. Though not the most prestigious of tournaments (10,000 being the best pre-final attendance), Wembley is Wembley, so few of the 68,000 crowd complained about their day out, or the entertainment, as City lost a nine-goal thriller 4-5. This is City's squad for the Wembley final. From left to right, back row: Redmond, Clements, Nixon, McCarthy, Lillis. Middle row: McNab, May, Wilson, Baker, Moulden, Reid. Front row: Davies, Phillips, Power (captain), Melrose, Simpson. Standing: Frizzell (assistant manager), McNeil (manager), Bailey (trainer). Of this group, apart from skipper Power, only Steve Redmond 283 (4), Kenny Clements 276 (6), Neil McNab 261 (5), and Nicky Reid 256 (6) would play over 250 matches for the club. More upheaval would soon follow!

In September 1986 McNeil resigned
and Jimmy Frizzel replaced him.
Everyone knew performances had to
improve, but just eight wins resulted in
relegation again. A new manager
arrived, this time Mel Machin, and as in
City's previous Division Two stint it
would take two seasons to reclaim top-
flight status. One game eclipsed all
others though – City's clash with
Huddersfield Town. No spectator
present will ever forget the result, which
was an astonishing 10-1, or Paul
Stewart, Tony Adcock and David
White's hat-tricks. This is the match
programme from this record-breaking
game.

David White scores number ten against Huddersfield. Strong, fast and exciting, David progressed from City's successful youth team to win a cap for England. These days David summarises City matches on local radio. In all he appeared 328 (14) times for City, scoring 96 goals.

Left: City's match programme for the game against Watford recorded the Huddersfield achievement on its front cover with a picture of the three hat-trick heroes. *Below:* Inside, this headline says it all!

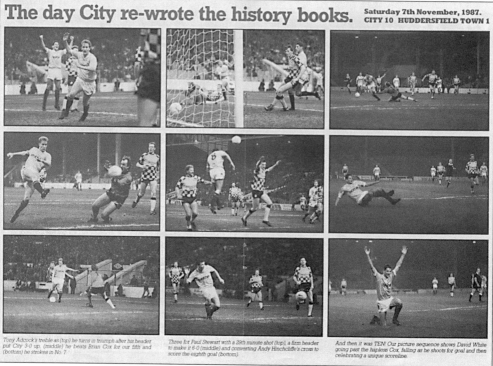

The day City re-wrote the history books.

Saturday 7th November, 1987.
CITY 10 HUDDERSFIELD TOWN 1

Tony Adcock's treble as (top) he turns in triumph after his header put City 3-0 up, (middle) he beats Brian Cox for our fifth and (bottom) he strokes in No. 7.

Three for Paul Stewart with a 26th minute shot (top), a firm header to make it 6-0 (middle) and converting Andy Hinchcliffe's cross to score the eighth goal (bottom).

And then it was TEN! Our picture sequence shows David White going past the hapless Cox, falling as he shoots for goal and then celebrating a unique scoreline.

Above: Manchester City FC, 1988/89. From left to right, back row: Moulden, Morley, Biggins, Gleghorn, Deehan, Hinchcliffe, Scott. Middle row: Machin (manager), Gayle, White, Dibble, Seagrave, Lake, Bailey (physiotherapist), Frizzell (assistant manager). Front row: McNab, Simpson, Redmond, Brightwell and Beckford. *Right*: For the majority of the 1988/89 season, City were in control of their destiny; one fifteen-match run in particular underpinning the campaign. Promotion would have been secured if they had won their last two home fixtures, but both games were drawn. City eventually celebrated their return to Division One in the last match of the season with a 1-1 draw at Bradford City, Trevor Morley scoring the vital goal. The *Manchester Evening News* produced this special edition to mark the achievement.

BARCLAYS LEAGUE
DIVISION ONE

OFFICIAL MATCH MAGAZINE · £1

CITY

OFFICIAL CLUB SPONSORS.
brother
The future at your fingertips.

CITY v MANCHESTER UNITED
Saturday, 23rd September, 1989. Kick-off: 3.00 p.m.

The 1980s ended with the team bottom of Division One, and with yet another new manager, Howard Kendall, who was installed during December '89. Prior to this, amongst ten defeats was the club's worst for thirty years – 0-6 at Derby – yet perversely they experienced their best result against Manchester United since 1955. This is the match programme from the memorable derby match.

The referee points to the halfway line to signal a goal, as David Oldfield celebrates the first of his brace in the 5-1 hammering of United.

Andy Hinchcliffe is joined by Paul Lake after heading City's fifth goal of the game.

Kendall's appointment brought an immediate improvement and when City faced United again confidence had been restored. By April, safety had been achieved. This shot shows Ian Brightwell celebrating his goal in a 1-1 draw at Old Trafford. Brightwell, a member of City's 1986 Youth Cup winning team, was a regular for many years and made a total of 337 (45) appearances, scoring 19 goals.

Manchester City FC, 1990/91. From left to right, back row: David White, Paul Lake, Andy Dibble, Niall Quinn, Tony Coton, Colin Hendry, Mark Seagraves. Middle row: Roy Bailey (physiotherapist), Tony Book (coach), Ian Brightwell, Alan Harper, Neil Pointon, Clive Allen, Ashley Ward, Wayne Clarke, Gary Megson, Michael Heaton (assistant manager). Front row: Adrian Heath, Mark Brennan, Peter Reid, Howard Kendall (manager), Steve Redmond, Jason Beckford, Mark Ward. Kendall rocked City in November 1990 by rejoining Everton, Peter Reid taking over as player-manager within nine days. The change proved a blessing as the team finished fifth, their highest placing since 1978. The most impressive performance of the season came at Villa Park where City destroyed their opponents 5-1 (White grabbing four of the goals).

In 1991/92 City again finished fifth, with Tony Coton and Keith Curle their most consistent performers. City reserved their best form for the back-to-back Easter clashes against title contenders Leeds and Manchester United. Old Trafford virtually had the champagne corks popping after City's 4-0 demolition of Leeds (above) on 4 April, but three days later a Curle penalty (below) swung the title-race open again (which Leeds won after United capitulated at the very death).

City's form dipped at the onset of the Premier League, but few supporters could understand the logic in Peter Reid's dismissal after just four fixtures. Brian Horton took over within two days of Reid's departure, but the team struggled, finishing just three points above the drop-zone. Their best result came at Stamford Bridge, where shown here, Mike Sheron salutes travelling supporters after scoring his second goal in City's 4-2 win. Rick Holden joins him in his celebrations.

In 1993/94 City again just avoided relegation. The biggest problem was a lack of goals, due mainly to Quinn's long-term absence through injury and White's departure to Leeds. Indeed, City's top League scorer, Mike Sheron, managed just 6 – the lowest seasonal return for the leading marksman in the club's history. Off the field Francis Lee finally replaced Peter Swales as chairman. Here, Quinn is seen in action against Liverpool before his injury. A fine leader of the line, many fans were sorry to see Quinn depart after scoring 78 goals in his 219 (25) appearances for the club.

City got off to a reasonable start in 1994/95, but four wins in their last twenty-five games left them only just safe in seventeenth place. *Above*: Uwe Rosler slots home one of his two goals in the team's 4-0 win against Everton. *Below*: Niall Quinn notches his first League goal since injury in City's 5-2 thrashing of Tottenham.

The matches that ultimately brought safety in 1994/95 came at Easter when City surprised everyone by beating Liverpool, who finished fourth, and Champions-elect Blackburn Rovers. This photograph shows three Liverpool players watching helplessly as Gaudino strikes the winning goal in City's 2-1 win. Also in shot is City's Nicky Summerbee (16), who like his father played on the wing during 142 (14) appearances for the club.

Keith Curle calmly slots home a penalty in City's brilliant 3-2 triumph at Ewood Park. A cultured, yet at times ruthless, defender, Curle played 203 matches for City.

Manchester City FC, 1995/96. From left to right, back row: Rae Ingram, Ian Brightwell, Garry Flitcroft, Nathan Freeman, Michel Vonk, Alan Kernaghan, Steve Lomas. Middle row: Neil McNab (youth team manager), Les Chapman (reserve team coach), Scott Thomas, Nick Summerbee, John Foster, Tony Coton, Andy Dibble, Paul Lake, Uwe Rosler, Keith Curle, Tony Book (first team coach), Asa Hartford (assistant manager). Front row: Roy Bailey (physiotherapist), Niall Quinn, Terry Phelan, Georgiou Kinkladze, Alan Ball (manager), Peter Beagrie, Paul Walsh, Richard Edghill, Ronnie Evans (assistant physiotherapist). Survival had failed to save Horton his job, Alan Ball replacing him during the close season. Ball's first signing from Dynamo Tiblisi was inspirational and soon became the hero of Maine Road…Kinkladze had arrived.

City made a dreadful start in 1995/96, gaining just two points from their opening eleven matches, yet they controlled their destiny to the very end. One of just nine victories came in a 2-1 win over Southampton. This action shot shows two-goal hero Kinkladze skipping away from a challenge in a match that he totally dominated – his winning strike certainly won't be forgotten by City fans.

With just three games remaining, Rosler scored the only goal against Sheffield Wednesday to keep hopes alive. Steve Lomas (right) then scored the vital goal at Villa Park in another 1-0 win.

In the final match of the season at home to Liverpool, City went two behind, but staged a wonderful comeback to level the scores. Lomas is seen here congratulating Kit Symons on his equaliser. As the clock ran down Ball mistakenly believed a point would be sufficient for safety and he instructed his players to hold for a draw. By the time the correct information was relayed it was too late...City were relegated by an inferior goal difference, having finished on the same points as Southampton and Coventry.

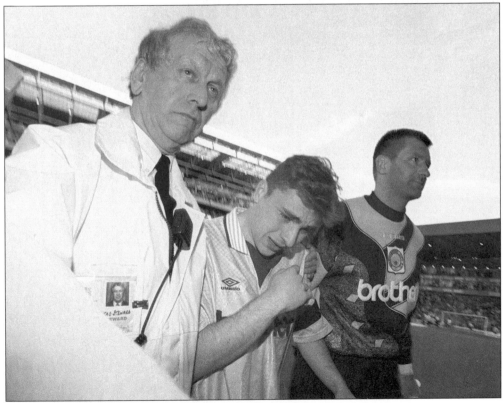

Many cried on 5 May 1996, including Georgie Kinkladze.

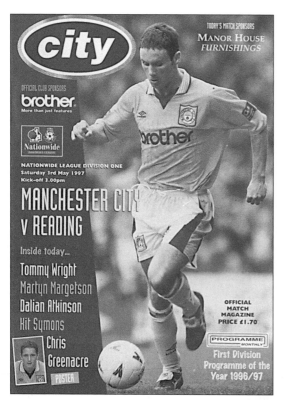

The hangover from relegation continued, and most blamed Ball, who resigned three matches into the 1996/97 season. The shenanigans that followed in a quest for a new manager was ridiculous as four appointments took place within four months! Initially, Asa Hartford stood in as caretaker-manager before Steve Coppell's appointment on 7 October. Coppell lasted just thirty-two days, stating stress as his reason for resignation. Phil Neal then became caretaker number two before finally Frank Clark took over on 28 December. By now City had only three clubs below them in Division One, but inspired by Clark went on an unbeaten nine-match run that enabled them to finish in mid-table. Uwe Rosler top-scored for a third consecutive season with 15 League goals. This is a match programme from the clash with Reading in May 1997.

City were promotion favourites in 1997/98, but the pundits were proved dramatically wrong as the players produced just twelve wins, the last in the final game at Stoke where both teams dropped into Division Two. At the lowest point in the club's history, one matter was assured – the man charged with reviving the team's fortunes would be Joe Royle, who had been appointed the previous February. This is the match programme from the game with Oxford United in March 1998.

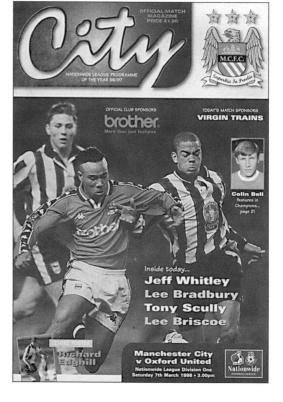

Relegation may have been a disaster…but once a blue always a blue. Crowds poured into Maine Road and away games became opponents' match of the season as far as the gate money was concerned. Incredibly home attendances actually went up following the drop into the lower half of the League structure! Although City were thereabouts throughout the campaign, it was a run of nine wins in the last thirteen games that clinched a play-off spot. Wigan stood in their way of the play-off final and in the first leg the players were happy with a 1-1 draw, Paul Dickov scoring. In the return a capacity crowd witnessed a nerve-jangling affair where a single Shaun Goater effort proved sufficient. *Above:* A match ticket from the return clash with Wigan. *Right:* The match programme for the crucial game.

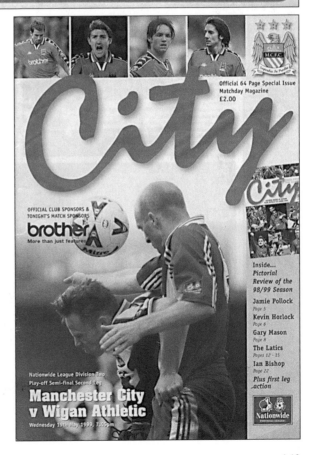

Official 64 Page Special Issue
Matchday Magazine
£2.00

OFFICIAL CLUB SPONSORS & TONIGHT'S MATCH SPONSORS
brother
More than just features

Inside…
Pictorial Review of the 98/99 Season
Jamie Pollock
Page 5
Kevin Horlock
Page 6
Gary Mason
Page 8
The Latics
Pages 12 - 15
Ian Bishop
Page 22
Plus first leg action

Nationwide League Division Two
Play-off Semi-final Second Leg
Manchester City v Wigan Athletic
Wednesday 19th May 1999, 7.45pm

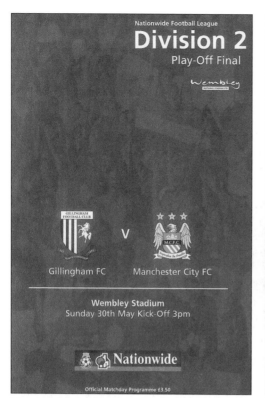

Here are a match programme, ticket and rosette from the play-off final with Gillingham. Note which teams the organisers thought would reach Wembley on the match ticket!

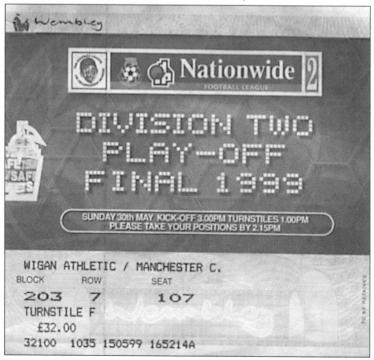

76,935 fans crammed into Wembley stadium for a match that would test the emotions like no other. Two goals down with five minutes remaining...surely it's over according to the expressions on City's bench.

Firstly a Horlock goal after 89 minutes made it 1-2...then Dickov (above) scored after 94 minutes to level the scores at 2-2. As chairman David Bernstein commented later, 'our equalising goal will always send a tingle down the spine of City fans'. It was then time for penalties!

Cooke, Horlock and Edghill had all converted their spot-kick and the score was 3-1. It was then up to Nicky Weaver, who saved Gillingham's fourth penalty to secure promotion...before eventually being swamped! City had achieved what seemed impossible after 85 minutes.

It was party time for jubilant fans and players alike.

Pundits predicted stability for Manchester City in 1999/2000 – but not Joe's boys, as fourteen wins in the opening twenty matches pushed them into the melting pot for promotion again. A sticky seven-match run without a win during February and March raised doubts, but all questions were emphatically answered with six wins in their remaining eight matches. City were on the brink of a return to the Premier League. *Above*: The match programmes from City's opening and last home fixtures of the season. *Below*: Robert Taylor celebrates his strike that gave City a vital win over Birmingham City in the penultimate game of the season.

Blackburn Rovers Millennium Season 1999-2000
our goals are yours

NATIONWIDE LEAGUE DIVISION ONE

B.R.F.C. v MANCHESTER CITY

07/05/2000   TIME 13:30

JACK WALKER STAND UPPER TIER

AREA COLOUR - "MAGENTA"

T/STILE	ROW	SEAT	PRICE
M	8	26	£18.00

ADULT

MR DJ TAYLOR 11677

Ticket Office **Freephone** 08080 10 10 10   TO BE RETAINED FOR FUTURE MATCH APPLICATIONS

Just one match left: away to Blackburn Rovers. A win would mean that City were back in the big time of the Premier League. This is a precious match ticket from the encounter.

ARTE ET LABORE

ALBION ROAD
CAR PARK Nº

DATE 07-05-00

VERSUS MAN CITY

CIS
OFFICIAL CLUB SPONSOR

BLACKBURN ROVERS FC EWOOD PARK

MATCH DAY PASS

A car park pass from Ewood Park.

The teams walk out at Ewood Park clearly fired up.

After Blackburn had taken a first half lead, leading goalscorer Shaun Goater equalised with his 23rd of the season.

By the time Paul Dickov celebrated his effort the match was over, following a Dailly own goal and a Mark Kennedy effort. Nonetheless this was a sweet moment.

After a four-year absence Manchester City were back where they belonged.

We've done it!

Nicky Weavers' expression says it all! Nicky is continuing the City tradition of producing first-class 'keepers. A £100,000 signing from Mansfield Town, he made his debut in a friendly against Jamaica and hasn't looked back since. The current England under-21 goalkeeper, many tip him to go all the way.

The men who masterminded City's return, Joe Royle and David Bernstein, embrace after the crucial match...Premier League football here we come!

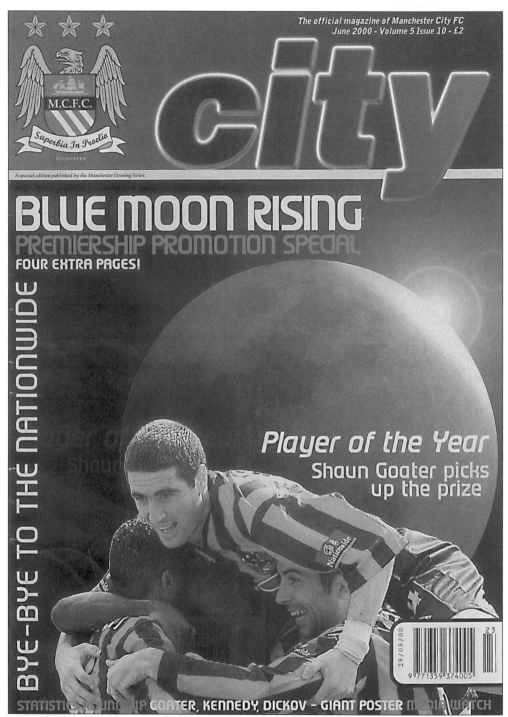

The club's official magazine marked City's most recent achievement with this publication. For supporters and players alike the new season couldn't come soon enough.